A quiet French country district is the site of a nuclear waste reprocessing plant. Françoise Zonabend describes the ways in which those working in the plant, and living nearby, come to terms with the risks in their daily lives. She provides a superb sociology of the nuclear work-place, with its divisions and hierarchies, and explains the often unexpected responses of the workers to the fear of irradiation and contamination. The work is described euphemistically in terms of women's tasks – cleaning, cooking, preparing a soup – but the male workers subvert this language to create a more satisfying self-image. They divide workers into the cautious *rentiers* and the bold *kamikazes*, who relish danger. By analysing work practices and the language of the work-place, the author shows how workers and locals can recognise the possibility of nuclear catastrophe while, at the same time, denying that it could ever happen to them. This is a major contribution to the anthropology of modern life.

The nuclear peninsula

The nuclear peninsula

Françoise Zonabend

Translated from the French by J. A. Underwood

CAMBRIDGE
UNIVERSITY PRESS

Editions de la Maison des Sciences de l'Homme

Published by the Press Syndicate of the University of Cambridge
The Pitt Building, Trumpington Street, Cambridge CB2 1RP
40 West 20th Street, New York, NY 10011–4211, USA
10 Stamford Road, Oakleigh, Victoria 3166, Australia
and Editions de la Maison des Sciences de l'Homme
54 Boulevard Raspail, 75270 Paris Cedex 06

Originally published in French as *La presqu'île au nucléaire*
by Editions Odile Jacob 1989
and © Editions Odile Jacob, Novembre 1989
First published in English by Editions de la Maison des Sciences de l'Homme and
Cambridge University Press 1993 as *The nuclear peninsula*
English translation © Maison des Sciences de l'Homme and Cambridge University
Press 1993

Printed in Great Britain at the University Press, Cambridge

A catalogue record for this book is available from the British Library

Library of Congress cataloguing in publication data

ISBN 0 521 41321 4 hardback
ISBN 2 7351–0478–8 hardback (France only)

CE

Contents

Illustrations

Preface

Once there was a landscape ...

This book deals with the everyday lives of people who work in or live near high-risk industrial establishments. To study this subject, I took the case of the nuclear industry, centring my research on the spent nuclear fuel reprocessing plant at la Hague on the western tip of the Cotentin Peninsula in Normandy.

It was the award of a research contract by the Social Sciences Commission of the French Ministry of the Environment in 1987 that prompted me to undertake a monograph on the plant, though I had actually begun thinking about it as far back as 1980, while on a visit to the region. Struck by the beauty of this coastal landscape and the harmony and silence of its little *villages* (in Norman dialect usage, really hamlets) tucked away down leafy lanes, I decided to stop there and do some ethnographic research. I was aware from the outset of the presence, up on the plateau a mile or so inland from these untamed shores, of a nuclear facility of some kind and of the fact that a second was being built alongside the first. I had even driven along the road that borders the site. However, though I had passed quite close I had either not noticed it or not wished to notice it. Nor did the people (residents of long standing, some local councillors) whom I approached to find out whether I might come and live at la Hague ever mention it to me. The upshot was that I decided to go ahead, found a house overlooking the sea, moved in, and forgot all about the plant.

Time passed, and it was not until several months later that I thought again about the industrial buildings springing up in increasing numbers on the plateau right behind my house. That was when I became conscious of the fact that in this place two opposing worlds existed side by side. Coming and going between Paris and this spot at the back of beyond, I found that a fresh surprise greeted me on each return. Yet I never lost the sense of the perenniality of my new surroundings. In the few weeks of my absence, certain areas would have changed utterly; others, by contrast, remained immutable, as if frozen in time.

Combing la Hague in search of a particular type of genealogical memory or in an attempt to find out how its people organised and operated their kinship networks (these being the pegs on which I intended to hang my ethnographic research), I visited house after house in the many *villages* that lie concealed in the little valleys notching the edge of the plateau. Here farmers and fishermen live by the rhythm of the seasons and the tides. In narrow streets that seem always to be deserted, between high stone walls overhung by camellias or mimosas, the only sound you hear is that of the water rushing down the gutter. A feeling of great calm descends on you in these silent hamlets. And when you enter one of the dwellings, where a wood fire burns all year round in the tall fireplace in the communal room, tended by an old woman kneeling on the stone hearth in ancestral pose, time does indeed stand still.

But walk only a few hundred yards farther and that tranquillity is shattered. Up on the plateau a broad boulevard has been carved out to ease the flow of traffic. Lorries pass at the rate of one every three minutes; private cars form a constant flood from eight in the morning till five in the evening, causing endless jams. And there, at the end of the road, looms the plant, a veritable city deposited in the middle of the countryside, ringed by a triple fence of electrified barbed wire, with a watchtower guarding the entrance. Ranged over the plateau beyond the wire is a series of concrete buildings with blank façades and, shooting skywards between the giant cranes, enormously tall chimneys with corkscrew flanges. Farther off, curious-looking high walls of concrete shafts piled one on top of another adorn the landscape between the circular domes of strange tumuli. All is noise and bustle, crashing, roaring, and confusion. These men are constructing the world's most modern nuclear plant on the biggest building site in Europe.

At first it was the juxtaposition of these dissonant spheres that I wanted to describe, the tension between these two worlds, one locked in a remote past, the other wide open to the technology of the future. How is it possible, I wanted to know, for two apparently so irreconcilable extremes to coexist in the same setting?

I also wanted to throw light, if I could, on the silences, the omissions, the memory lapses that *le nucléaire* (the conveniently concise French expression that covers every aspect of the technology based on nuclear fission; Tr.) occasions in such places – and which afflict me, too, when I am in residence at la Hague.

So I tried to find out how people behave, living alongside such high-risk establishments: do they accept them, reject them, dream about them; are they willing to talk about them? Can they in fact talk about them?

Finally, focusing on the men and women who actually work at the plant and are daily confronted with the invisible but ubiquitous presence of radioactivity, I attempted to understand how they react to it, how they think about it, and how they experience it. What is the nature of their relationship with this energy whose dangerous effects are so unpredictable, this phenomenon that they need to make a deliberate conceptual effort to locate within their own grids of interpretation?

The research underlying the present work was done under the auspices of the Laboratoire d'Anthropologie sociale, a combined unit of the Centre national de la Recherche scientifique and the Ecole des Hautes Etudes en Sciences sociales in association with the Collège de France. It was funded by the Social Sciences Commission of the Service de la Recherche des Etudes et de Traitment de l'Information sur l'Environnement, a department of the Ministry of the Environment and of Protection against Major Natural and Technological Risks. Part of it was undertaken by Pierre Paris, holder of a DEA in sociology from the University of Caen, who was particularly interested in studying the kinds of social change that have taken place in the villages. His study is entitled *Vivre l'espace à la Hague* ('La Hague as living-space').

Abbreviations

ACRO	Association pour la contrôle de la radioactivité dans l'Ouest
ANDRA	Agence nationale pour la gestion des dechets radioactif
CCPAH	Comité contre la pollution atomique dans la Hague
CEA	Commissariat à l'Energie atomique
CFDT	Confédération française démocratique du travail
CIAT	Comité interministériel d'aménagement du territoire
COGEMA	Compagnie générale des matières nucléaires
CRILAN	Comité régional d'information et de luttes anti-nucléaires
EDF	Electricité de France
HAO	Haute Activité Oxyde
PWR	Pressurised-water reactor
SCPRI	Service centrale de protection contre les rayonnements ionisants
SGN	Saint-Gobain nucléaire, former name of the Société des Techniques nouvelles, principal contractor of the *Grand chantier*
TDA/TNA/TNDA	Travailleurs directement affectés/Travailleurs non-affectés/Travailleurs non directement affectés (en zone radioactive)
UP2, UP3	Usines (Unités) de production de plutonium

Introduction   Talking nuclear

The only way to access those grids of interpretation is to attempt to 'talk nuclear' with local inhabitants and with people who work at the plant. Accordingly, I was led in the course of my researches to pay most attention to the act of speech. That is to say, I conducted the study mainly through live interviews, either with individuals or with groups, always making due allowance for the context in which the enunciative act took place. Indeed, that act must never be considered in isolation from the circumstances in which it is performed, from the place where it occurs, or from the social and professional identity of the speaker or speakers. A further characteristic is that it sets up an interaction with the interlocutor (the interviewer), locating each party within a network of relationships that itself requires decoding. Adopting this approach involves as it were taking all the material available to you and incorporating it in your analysis of a person's speech: the combinative aspect of discourse sequences, the use of certain words rather than others, the position and weight of silences, the proportions of narratable and memorisable elements in the conduct of the account, the inflections introduced by the reflexive nature of narrative exchange.

There is quite rightly a big question mark over the soundness of such an approach when the area under investigation covers everyday practices to which people resort unthinkingly and in connection with which their speech is necessarily forgetful, or when the researcher is trying to capture thoughts, feelings, and private, secret areas of behaviour that people likewise find difficult to express in speech. In my opinion, however, it is the only course.

There is also the fact that in this context your own speech as interviewer, as ostensibly impartial, neutral observer, constitutes a source of provocation, both politically and psychologically.

At la Hague, more than anywhere else in France (though this is noticeable to a greater or lesser extent in every region where high-risk establishments are located), a person conducting a study of the social and psychological implications of the installation of nuclear sites is immediately looked upon as an opponent of nuclear power. Neutrality on this point simply will not wash. The economic fortunes and political equilibrium of the region are bound up with the maintenance and development of its nuclear industries. Asking questions about the safety of such installations or about the whole range of problems encountered by those who live near them or work in them inspires instant distrust and puts you straight in the 'anti' bracket every time.

How do people talk about it?

It stands to reason, perhaps, that if a person is to live in conditions of tolerable moral comfort he does not wish to keep reminding himself or being reminded of the fact that he inhabits a special sort of place and works in a dangerous establishment. Naturally, no one wants to subject himself to questions on the subject. If he lives there, if he works there, it is because the risk to him is nil. Consequently, any question about danger incurred or risks run will be rejected, denied, or parried in some way. People who interview populations living in the vicinity of nuclear power stations are well aware of this phenomenon: every poll ever published shows that, the nearer people live to a nuclear power station, the more they will swear by its reliability.[1] Similarly, those who observe workers in high-risk industries are familiar with the way in which they refuse to acknowledge the dangers of their job to the point where it is hard to get them to admit to taking essential safety precautions.[2]

In the nuclear industry there is no question of anyone refusing to accept the dangers of radioactivity or of working in a radioactive environment. The effects of nuclear energy are too well-known for that. If the risk is denied or defied, it is because in this place every precaution is taken.

True, in France the civil nuclear industry is undoubtedly the most closely monitored area of industrial activity. The safety of nuclear installations and that of the people working in them and living alongside them are matters that have been taken into consideration from the outset. Furthermore, those installations are constantly being reviewed and fresh safety demands formulated. As we shall see, a combination of historical events, the prominent part played by one trade union in particular,[3] and considerations of a political nature accounts for so coherent a body of arrangements having been put in place in this domain so far as France is concerned.

At la Hague a close watch is kept on the air, the rain, the sea water, the fauna and flora, the ground water, the cows' milk, and the flesh of shellfish in the area around the plant. Samples are taken and measures implemented by the plant's own Radioprotection Department and by the Central Department for Protection Against Ionising Radiation

(*Service central de protection contre les rayonnements ionisants* or SCPRI), which comes under the Ministry of Health, and the results are sent annually to the mayors of all the municipalities (*communes*) of the canton.

Staff at nuclear establishments undergo medical examinations at more or less frequent intervals, depending on the section of the plant they work in. No one is exempt. The results of those examinations and analyses are sent to the people concerned.

So, if every precaution has been taken, how shall a person *admit* or even *think* that he is still in any danger, and why, in any case, should he wrestle, whether actually or psychologically, with a risk that is improbable in the extreme? Certainly far less probable, at all events, than such everyday risks as driving a car, which everyone takes and thinks nothing of. This is why every question about danger incurred elicits the response that it is safer working at the plant or living nearby than getting the car out each morning.

The spoken word, in this context, becomes a vehicle for any number of ruses designed to obscure the ostensible, purported meaning of the narrative heard. Language may tell or leave untold, guide or mislead, shed light or spread confusion. Many times in such accounts what is really being said hides itself away behind words intended to mask it. A whole set of stratagems is deployed with the single aim of creating opacity and ambiguity. The end result is that what finds expression in a roundabout way is a buried request, symptomatic of an inexpressible distress.

Let us look at some examples. If you ask technicians directly about the jobs they do in the plant and about the risks to which they are exposed when entering radioactive areas or handling ionising products, they reply readily enough, it is true, but they do so in a wholly remote, impersonal way, using technical terminology in an ostensibly 'scientific' type of utterance very like that found in current publications dealing with this type of work. It is unusual for them to talk spontaneously about their own experience, or their apprenticeship, or any incidents in which they may have been involved. In other words, the everyday reality of their jobs seems to be something they cannot talk about, and perhaps it is. They have, as it were, a ready-made discourse for answering questions. In fact, it sometimes struck me as pointless noting down what they said, since they always handed out the same old thing. What, indeed, is the point of taking down a lesson that somebody reels off without a single mistake, that is identical to the one you can read in the official scientific brochures, and that in the circumstances merely confirmed that the people I was interviewing *knew* what they could expect?

However, if, as was invariably the case, all questions bearing directly on incidents that might have happened to the interviewee were parried or obscured in this way by a scientific discourse, it is reasonable to suppose that what is involved here is a way of the speaker not saying or not hearing himself say something he wishes to conceal.

Throughout this study it was as if none of the technicians I met had ever been the victim of an incident involving radioactivity. Incidents occur daily, in fact, but 'trouble' occurred only to others, never to those I was speaking to, as if for one reason or another they were unable to tell me about the *histoires* that had concerned them. Never did their words convey anything of the personal, private side of their experiences. By means of enunciative tactics of this kind the field of anxiety was continually being manipulated and reshaped.

However, in such accounts of lives spent entirely in the service of *le nucléaire*, there will sometimes be a moment of hesitation, often towards the end of the interview when the talk is more relaxed, more familiar. I am on my feet, about to leave, the tape-recorder is switched off, when the interviewee, extricating himself from his militant role or dropping his guard of scientific language, voices or rather murmurs (as if I were not there) one or two thoughts that offer a glimpse of the fear and moral anguish he keeps constantly suppressed. For instance, I recall a conversation with one technician who had worked at the plant for fifteen years, a militant trade unionist who spent more than two hours telling me about the reliability of the equipment at *his* plant and maintaining that he worked there in complete safety. Then, at the very end of our conversation, as if to redress the balance in some way after all the rationalisations, he abruptly treated me to certain confidences, as it were, about cancer, about how he might be threatened by it, and about how, should he ever contract the disease, it would prevent him from enjoying his retirement. This made him wonder whether, in the circumstances, it was necessary to spend one's entire life in the service of an industry in which worker safety could never be totally guaranteed.

Exactly the same oscillations in speech, swinging from peremptory affirmation regarding the safety of nuclear establishments to anxious questions about the risks to which those same establishments expose whole populations, are found among the people of la Hague. Take the mayor of one municipality, so fervent a supporter of the nuclear industry that the management of the plant once sent him to Japan to persuade the inhabitants of a region soon to have its own French-built reprocessing plant that living in the vicinity of such an establishment is a cinch. Nevertheless, at the end of our conversation (which he had not wanted me to record on tape), having extolled the benefits that the village communally and he personally derived from the presence of the plant, he broke off and was silent for a moment before resuming:

> I want the truth ... The truth means knowing which is right: are small doses dangerous, or are they not? You have those on the one hand who would eat limpets that had been living in the pipe[4] for six months and others who wouldn't eat them for anything in the world. Who's right? Who's telling the truth? It's incredible! No one can give me an answer ... You ... Do you know what the truth is?[5]

I learned later that, his avowed beliefs notwithstanding, he refused to eat any fish or shellfish caught off the coasts of la Hague.

Linguistic analysis may take place at many other levels. For example, you can study the forms of communication between the management of the plant and the public. Here, people's utterances distinguish two spheres: one that *knows* (the management) and one that *does not know* (the public). Between these two worlds there is a play of forces in which it is words that take the strain. Some (those who know) declare that their words are the truth; the rest have always felt that those same words are being used to deceive, to travesty the truth. Hence this remark by one local politician: 'When "they" [he meant the management] don't want people to understand, they talk in technical terms.'

Communication between these two worlds is like nothing so much as the interplay of distorting mirrors.

Taking the words at face value

So it was the act of speech rather than direct observation (or any other method, for that matter; they are all more or less inappropriate in this kind of industrial context) that struck me as capable of providing information about this particular individual and collective experience. Speech, or perhaps I should say oral expression, with its digressions, censorships, intonations, and metaphorical substitutions (in a word, rhetoric), affords the possibility of exposing the processes of deletion, spotting defensive tactics, and generally identifying the thousand and one ways in which people seek to confound anxiety. Speech needs to be interpreted, of course, and in this case the business of interpretation consisted essentially in an attempt to take the words spoken at their face value. But it was also, on occasion, a matter of seeking an understanding beyond the words or by stopping short of the words in order to flush out the implicit meaning behind the ostensible content.

It was in fact in their changes of direction, in the flaws in their arguments, and in the interstices of their speech that our interviewees did, willy-nilly, reveal something of themselves and allow a latent anxiety to show through. To an even greater extent it was in slips, puns, and instances of misappropriation of vocabulary as well as in metaphor and in the workings of the imagination that one glimpsed a real anxiety that was being denied by these people in their preoccupation with going on living and working in this place without suffering too much discomfort and self-questioning.

There are of course many other areas and many other manifestations in which this suppressed anxiety may be read.

I could, for example, have directed my attention towards the frantic consumption of organised sporting or leisure activities to the point where the free time of plant employees is always full, as if they were incapable of even a few moments' relaxation, alone with themselves. Granted, the general works council of the plant has a large budget at its disposal and has been able to mount a massive cultural and sporting programme.

'You can do twenty-six different sports here . . . On top of that, the plant is building a whole sports complex just for us in one of the villages nearby!' The speaker, a young technician who had recently been taken on, was citing one of the reasons why he had moved to la Hague.

Recently the management and the various works councils have set about creating a veritable works culture that will guarantee social harmony on the shop floor and peace of mind at home.

Then, too, there is the silence in which people who work at the plant bury the jobs they do on the site and the minor incidents that sometimes occur. Husbands or fathers will never talk about what they do there, and their wives and children all say they know nothing of what happens 'up there'. Moreover, no one dares to ask, neither the men's families, nor their friends, nor their relations. It is as if everyone respected the pact of silence that those who work at the plant have unwittingly imposed. The doctors and medical auxiliaries whom I met insisted that patients of theirs from the plant never ask them about the possibility of a link between what is currently wrong with them and the work they are required to do. It is just as if, on the one side as on the other, nobody wants to know. In this context of doubt and suppressed anxiety, but also of impotence in the face of a risk that no one can put his finger on, the only realistic stance is one of silence.

The researcher also needs to be attentive to the hundred and one rumours flying about on the subject of workers at the plant or what fate has in store for those who live on the threshold of this dangerous complex, wrapping the place in a web of muttered incantations and conjurations.

I might, with the same object in view, have tried to reach a better understanding of the language of looks, the unspoken dialogue that takes place between people when a siren goes off unexpectedly or an unfamiliar bang is heard from the direction of the plant. Or perhaps to grasp the significance of the absence of disaster dreams. Of the people I interviewed, all but two[6] assured me that they never had such dreams, as if everyone here unconsciously forbids him or herself to dream about a nuclear apocalypse. It would have meant, of course, finding out about the sorts of screening dreams that were blocking them out. But that would have been an enormous undertaking.

I observed, rubbed shoulders with, and analysed all these manifestations, whether collective or solitary, tiny or substantial, as well as others that were sometimes silent, sometimes obtrusive. They constitute as it were parallel languages that have the effect of enriching the utterances made in direct exchanges, like so many anonymous words adding their bit to those overtly uttered, omitted, or distorted, balancing them, qualifying them, directing their drift.

All these languages, be they silent or expressed, mumbled under the breath or articulated out loud, speak with one voice of a pain that cannot be denied, a buried anguish, a happiness lost for ever.

Whom do you talk to? Whom do you listen to?

I collected these words, these utterances, these silences in two ways.

Firstly, I had one or more conversations with the people of la Hague,[7] whether residents of long standing or recent arrivals and whether they worked at the plant or not. Naturally, I also requested interviews not only with everyone occupying any kind of position at the plant (manager, personnel manager, heads of departments, engineers, technicians, trade union representatives, doctors, welfare assistants, and the like) but also with people working in other establishments, whether connected with the nuclear industry or not. Such interviews might proceed along formal lines (complete with tape-recordings) or they might be highly informal and relaxed (conversations over meals to which I was invited). Similarly, I had many conversations (some spontaneous, some by appointment) with local residents: farmers, craft tradesmen, councillors, teachers, heads, schoolchildren, and so on. Since 1983, when I first became interested in the nuclear industry, I have conducted more than 150 interviews, either alone or accompanied by a colleague.

My second approach consisted in attending the training and refresher course[8] undergone by every new recruit to the la Hague plant and repeated by every technical operator after a few years of working there. An anonymous presence among the technicians, I listened to the demonstrations, followed the explanations, and watched the films shown for our benefit by the instructors. In so doing

I was able to grasp the way in which the scientific hierarchy interprets and presents the reality of the jobs that men and women are required to perform at la Hague on a daily basis. This gave me the opportunity of going to the sources of the technical language that was reproduced for me in the interviews and enabled me to assess the kinds of deflection, distortion, and adjustment that it undergoes in the process of solicited or spontaneous verbal exchange. Lastly I was able, through the apathy or interest shown by the trainees, to apprehend their behaviour and the way in which they think about and represent to themselves their relationship to the particular phenomenon – radio-activity – with which they were in constant contact.

Apart from the interviews with members of the plant management, which took place at the plant itself and consequently followed an agreed pattern, all the others sprang from a personal request without my exploiting any kind of official standing. It follows that a study of this type generates a spontaneous selection of the population studied because of the network of acquaintanceship that forms and fills out as the work progresses. You never visit anyone without having been recommended by other people whom you know already (in fact they may well accompany you). Of course, given this manner of proceeding, your work will resist all attempts to extract statistical representation of any sort, which may leave a question mark over any generalising interpretation (to which in any case I do not lay claim).

I saw a great many people, but I did not see everyone. The number of inhabitants or workers that I should have had to interview in order to obtain a minimum of representativeness for this milieu far exceeded the scope of the present study. Moreover, polls or brief questionnaires handled by anonymous investigators can never fill the bill when it comes to assessing everyday experience. The story of a person's life, elicited in the course of two, three, or four conversations with a trade union official, a militant ecologist, a technician at the plant, a local councillor, or a man or woman of la Hague will furnish a wealth of data that make more sense than a hundred replies to set questionnaires.

Furthermore, since in a place like la Hague the whole subject of *le nucléaire* is so provocative as to place anyone who raises it in the stereotyped 'anti-nuclear' bracket, there is inevitably something crucial about the kind of relationship that is established between interviewer and interviewee. It takes time for issues to become clarified on both sides. It takes time for the presence of the interviewer to cease to be a bone of contention and for a mutual relationship to become established in conversations solicited by him or her that will make it possible for both parties to go to the limits of what can be said. What, in such circumstances, would be the use of a remote, impersonal questionnaire?

Working in this way, you forget the obsession with being representative; you ignore quantitative observations in the attempt to capture emotional, irrational, imaginary elements, to apprehend all manner of aspects of reality and experience that, too often, slip through the net of so-called objective observation.

Part I
Nuclear landscapes

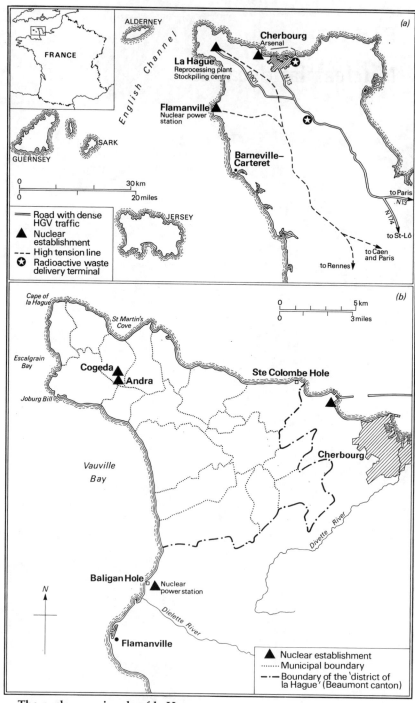

to Paris
N13
to St-Lô
to Caen
and Paris
to Rennes

(a)

ALDERNEY

FRANCE

English Channel

La Hague
Reprocessing plant
Stockpiling centre

Cherbourg
Arsenal

Flamanville
Nuclear power
station

**Barneville–
Carteret**

SARK

GUERNSEY

0   30 km
0   20 miles

JERSEY

—— Road with dense
     HGV traffic
▲ Nuclear
     establishment
- - - High tension line
✪ Radioactive waste
     delivery terminal

(b)

Cape of
la Hague

St Martin's
Cove

Escalgrain
Bay

Cogeda ▲
    ▲ **Andra**

Joburg Bill

Ste Colombe Hole

Vauville
Bay

Cherbourg

Divette River

Baligan Hole □
    ▲ Nuclear
      power station

N

Dielette River

• **Flamanville**

0   5 km
0   3 miles

▲ Nuclear establishment
······· Municipal boundary
—·—·— Boundary of the 'district of
         la Hague' (Beaumont canton)

The nuclear peninsula of la Hague

1 La Hague or the nuclear zone

A peninsula on the end of a peninsula, la Hague at the western extremity of the Cotentin is one of those in-between places. It neither belongs completely to the sea, nor is it wholly attached to the land. In fact, one would be hard put to it to say which element prevails here. Furthermore, depending on the criteria used to define it, different boundaries are assigned to the region. Geographically, la Hague is bounded on three sides by the sea and on the landward side by two rivers, the Divette and the Diélette, which rise within two kilometres of each other and enter the sea on different coasts: the former at Cherbourg, near the Swing Bridge, the latter at Flamanville on the west coast. Administratively and politically, la Hague consists of the present canton of Beaumont, the nineteen municipalities of which have been regrouped to form a single political entity known as 'le district de la Hague'. From the sociological point of view, the boundaries of la Hague are very much more fluid. Some say the 'real' la Hague is the remote area lying at the tip of the promontory beyond what is known as 'le Hague-Dicke', a huge earthwork that runs (or rather used to run, so severely have the actions of men and time damaged it in places) right across the peninsula from Gréville to Herqueville. Since in many Indo-European languages the word *Hague* does in fact mean 'hedge' or 'enclosure', it may in this case refer to the land originally bounded by the Hague-Dicke.[1] Be that as it may, for some people la Hague starts at Urville-Nacqueville; for others it starts at the Swing Bridge in Cherbourg, and for them 'past the bridge it's quite different, it's another world, it's la Hague'.

Whichever definition you take, however, there is general agreement about the peculiarities of the region. La Hague constitutes a distinct *pays*[2] alongside all the others that make up 'le Cotentin'.

Picture a harsh, wild stretch of nature with splendid horizons, endlessly fascinating in terms of the variety it offers to the eye. The interior of the peninsula is occupied by a great plateau consisting of a series of dome-like moors where gorse and broom, heather and bracken are swept by incessant wind. In places the plateau is cut by narrow valleys down which streamlets wind and where a few trees grow, their branches all drawn in one direction by the *vent d'amont*[3] that prevails for much of the year. Towards the northern coast the plateau drops down and the moor gives way to bare grassland punctuated by boulders and eroded outcrops and partitioned by low walls of flat stones sparsely dotted with vegetation. Towards the west the plateau terminates in towering cliffs that seem to drop straight into the sea. Farther south the moorland meets what are known locally as the *mielles*, huge hills of sand that the sea has thrown up between water and land.

And always, close by or at a distance, there is the sea, a sea that is rarely at rest but writhes with fearsome currents that ceaselessly mould the shore. The broad, clean sweep of Vauville Cove (*L'Anse de Vauville*), carpeted with sand and edged with dunes, gives way to the jagged red cliffs of Jobourg Bill (*Le Nez de Jobourg*), more than a hundred metres high, with escarpment after escarpment plunging endlessly into the sea. Beyond lies Ecalgrain Bay, an indentation in the curve of the cliffs bounded by two rocky promontories, and beyond that the Cape of la Hague itself, carved out of the low rocky coastline, with great stacks of rock rearing up at intervals, some attached to the land, others emerging from the sea, reminiscent of a ring of forbidding sentries keeping watch on the distant Channel Islands, which are just visible as mauve shadows on the horizon. It is at Jobourg Bill that the dangerous 'passage de la Déroute' ends and the 'raz Blanchard' begins, a terrible narrows in which the ebbing and flowing tides, forced between a series of reefs and shoals, reach speeds approaching nine knots.

This land of wind, rock, and water has scarcely proved favourable to human settlement. Those who do live here, however, have a formidable reputation. All the stories about la Hague agree in describing it as being peopled by tough, untamed individuals who, though they have little to say for themselves, are proud and clear-sighted. As if the soil, the climate, the whole natural environment of a place were believed to account for the character of the people who inhabited it! 'The Hagars [as the people of la Hague are called] were once famous throughout Normandy for their physical strength, ponderous movements, conspicuous indecisiveness, and slowness of wit, coupled with a genuine intelligence and a reliable and persevering nature.'[4]

It is also true that down the centuries the Hagars have gained a solid reputation as smugglers and wreckers and are for that reason regarded as folk well-suited to face perils whether old or new, real or imaginary.

Settlement is scattered in *villages* that are really hamlets consisting of a few houses grouped together. To escape the violence of the wind these either have their backs to the sea, nestle in little valleys, or take advantage of undulations in the inland plateau. Until recently the relatively small population (under 6,000 in 1975, equivalent to an average of forty inhabitants to the square kilometre) devoted the bulk of its energies to farming or seafaring pursuits. The coastline of la Hague has seen little development, and fishing has remained a coastal activity, traditionally practised in conjunction with agriculture or a craft trade. The population of fishermen has never been very great, nor has the fruit of their labours formed the object of any large-scale commercialisation. As for farming, what little land there is available has had to be wrested from the moor and is used primarily for growing grass and other fodder plants. Consequently, the peasant population has been declining steadily for the last hundred years.

Cut off, windswept, ringed by powerful ocean currents, unfit for any kind of economic development in terms of farming or fishing, doomed to depopulation – that was how geographers and historians used to describe la Hague up until the beginning of the 1960s. The selfsame reasons, however, made this the ideal site for an industrial complex dedicated to the reprocessing and stockpiling of spent nuclear fuel. If we include two further establishments flanking the base of the la Hague peninsula, namely the Flamanville nuclear power station and the Cherbourg Arsenal, where the nuclear-powered submarines are built, we have on this rocky promontory at the north-western edge of continental Europe France's greatest concentration of nuclear-related industries.

The nuclear triangle

On the eastern side of the peninsula, right on the outskirts of Cherbourg as you go towards la Hague, is the Arsenal. Established some 200 years ago, the Cherbourg Arsenal is administered by the Department of Naval Buildings and Armaments under the aegis of the 'Direction générale pour l'Armement'. It has specialised in submarine construction since the turn of the century, so it was the natural choice for building and testing the nuclear-powered and nuclear-armed submarines with which France decided to start equipping itself in 1960. Far and away the largest concern in the *département* (Manche), by 1 January 1987 the Cherbourg Arsenal was employing 4,800 persons, together with a further 700 or so on the payrolls of subcontractors.

Some twenty kilometres distant on the western side of the peninsula, at the other 'gateway' to la Hague, is the Flamanville nuclear power station. It occupies the site of the former Diélette underwater iron mines, opened up in 1866 and finally closed in 1962.

In 1977 France's national electricity board (*Electricité de France*, EDF) chose the spot for a nuclear power station. The two phases, delivering 1,265 megawatts each, came on stream in 1985 and 1986. The power station occupies 122 hectares (approximately 300 acres), half the area having been reclaimed from the sea. It provides jobs for around 550 people.

At the other end of Vauville Cove, up on the end of the plateau high above the sea, stand the buildings of the Spent Nuclear Fuel Reprocessing Plant (*Usine de retraitement des combustibles irradiés*). They sprawl over a site measuring 300 hectares (nearly 750 acres), entirely surrounded by three rows of fencing complete with barbed wire, chevaux-de-frise, and electrification.

The decision to construct it was made by the French Atomic Energy Commission (*Commissariat à l'Energie atomique*, CEA) in 1959. The idea was to treat the uranium fuel rods that have been 'burning' in the reactors of nuclear power stations for three years by extracting the plutonium and uranium still left in them and capable of being re-used for civil or military purposes.

Three years later, in 1962, the people of the region learned through the local press that a factory was to be built on the plateau of la Hague. Work began almost immediately, and France's second plutonium production plant (the first being situated at Marcoule, near Avignon) was commissioned in 1966. Ten years later the General Nuclear Substances Company (*Compagnie générale des matières nucléaires*, COGEMA), a public-interest company subject to private law and a wholly owned subsidiary of the CEA, acquired ownership of it and has run it ever since.

Designed and built to reprocess spent fuel from nuclear power stations with natural uranium/graphite/gas-cooled reactors, UP2 (as it came to be called) was modified in 1976 to enable it to reprocess on the one hand fuel from the light-water or pressurised-water reactors (PWR) adopted by EDF at that time and on the other hand fuel irradiated in Phénix reactors of the experimental fast-breeder type.[5] At the same time two new so-called High-Level Oxide workshops (*Haute Activité Oxyde*, HAO), HAO South and HAO North, were built on the site, making the plant multi-purpose and enabling it to access international nuclear-reprocessing markets. New outlets now opened up for the la Hague establishment, which decided in 1981 to build a second reprocessing unit (UP3) and to renovate the first. This second unit, with a productive capacity of 800 (metric) tons a year, is on the point of completion as I write (in 1989; the final completion date for UP3 is now 1992). Some of the shops are currently undergoing active trials, and virtually all the staff required to operate the unit efficiently have already been taken on. The renovation of UP2 consists in adding to or replacing the equipment of the present plant in order to boost its productive capacity from 400 to 800 tons a year. Also under construction is a third liquid-effluent purification station (*Station d'épuration des effluents liquides*, STE3) required for the evacuation of waste water from the new units (see map, p. 74).

This work is being done over a ten-year period (from 1981 to 1991) and has been largely financed in advance by the 'thirty electricity companies from six foreign countries that have signed reprocessing contracts with COGEMA in respect of 7,000 (metric) tons to be reprocessed over ten years'.[6] This point is frequently on the lips of members of the COGEMA management, who never fail to add: 'The plant is costing us nothing, you see – foreigners are paying for it . . . '

So two kinds of activity are going on simultaneously on the la Hague site. The first consists in operating and maintaining the UP2 reprocessing plant and those UP3 shops that have already been commissioned; the second comprises the construction work involved in building the new reprocessing units. Though very much interconnected, the two areas of activity are physically separated on the site by the so-called 'green fence', a barrier of wire netting surmounted by strands of barbed wire. As each UP3 workshop is completed, the green fence is moved in such a way as to bring it within the area managed directly by COGEMA, which then initiates what are known as 'live trials' (using radioactive material). These movements of the fence have given rise to a joke among the construction workers: they're not afraid of *le nucléaire*, they say, because 'the fence stops the radiation'!   This kind of facetiousness is in frequent use at la Hague, as we shall see, its irony simultaneously cloaking fears that cannot be admitted and conveying people's awareness of human impotence when it comes to providing anything more than a derisory protection against this phenomenon.

The plant and the construction site (referred to as the 'Grand chantier') have separate entrances. Everything is thus designed to keep the first sort of activity, namely operating the plant, distinct from the work of construction, confirming in everyone's eyes that *le nucléaire* constitutes a closed world, a world apart, almost, as it were, a forbidden world. It is also true that the work of extending the plant has required some 5,000 workers to come on to the site daily (throughout the peak period from 1985 to 1989) in addition to the 3,000 employed at UP2 and UP3. Every day something like 10,000 people use the single access road to converge on the la Hague site, and it became a matter of necessity somehow to organise the lives of these two populations working on the same site but in distinct sectors.

Once the two reprocessing units are in operation they will be staffed by some 3,100 persons, plus of course the sizeable outside workforce needed to meet the maintenance requirements of such establishments.

The la Hague complex reprocesses spent nuclear fuel. However, this is not something that can be recycled in its entirety. Once the various reprocessing operations have been completed, a certain amount of radioactive waste still remains, which then has to be treated and stockpiled.

There are two types of such waste. The first, known as 'high-level' waste, is a source of powerful radioactivity; it gives off a great deal of heat and goes on emitting highly dangerous radiation for a long time. This receives appropriate treatment *in situ*. Concentrated in aqueous solution, it is placed in stainless-steel tanks and stored in wells dug in the basement of the plant. A ventilation system keeps the wells cool. The hope is that as soon as possible such waste can be coated in vitreous material and transferred to storage sites hollowed out of particular rock formations and specially equipped for the purpose. However, the industrial phase of this process has yet to be perfected.

The other type, known as 'intermediate-level' waste, loses its radioactivity after some 300 years.[7] It is packed in metal drums and dispatched to the stockpiling facility adjacent to the site, which is managed by the National Agency for the Management of Radioactive Waste (*Agence nationale pour la gestion des déchets radioactifs*, ANDRA), a branch of the CEA. ANDRA occupies a twelve-hectare (thirty-acre) site on the la Hague plateau. Located next door to the plant, it receives not only the intermediate-level waste from la Hague but also all that produced by research departments, hospitals, and laboratories of all kinds. Its brief is to check the drums containing this very varied waste before compressing them and casting them in blocks of concrete. These are then stockpiled in concrete monoliths and buried in shallow graves or sunk in surface workings, forming tumuli that will subsequently be covered in layers of clay and topsoil. Opened in 1975, the ANDRA centre currently employs 120 persons; when it is full and closed down (supposedly in 1990, but for lack of alternative disposal sites ANDRA is still receiving waste today), two guards will be all that is needed to keep an eye on it.

In three hundred years' time this stockpiling area will, it is said, be restored to civilisation. If they wish to, people will be able to settle there.

In the space of twenty years this deserted, forgotten peninsula has thus undergone a process of intense industrialisation geared to a single type of technology: the exploitation of the atom. In less than a quarter of a century la Hague has emerged from the age of the plough and entered the nuclear era. An account of the installation of each of the establishments that now stand on the promontory will enable us to grasp in a tangible fashion the way in which the nuclear industry has taken possession of this region.

The nuclear era: first steps

Among the three establishments that mark out this 'nuclear tri-angle', the Cherbourg Arsenal is a special case. It comes under the state in the shape of the Defence Department (*Direction des forces militaires*), and as such its activities are covered by defence secrecy. Granted, the Arsenal workforce has a long tradition of industrial action (of a radical-socialist, never extremist persuasion), but its struggles have invariably been directed at improving working con-ditions and had nothing to do with the problem of nuclear safety. As one journalist explained:

> At the Arsenal, everything's secret. You're not allowed to take photo-graphs or go round the place. You never hear anything of accidents, even those that occur in the course of normal working. The Arsenal's military, and nothing must ever be allowed to leak out. Yet there they are, in the middle of town, handling radioactive products. What do they do with the waste? Lately they've been making a bit of an effort, issuing press releases about their activities and even organising an 'open day', though only for the families of Arsenal staff.

The Arsenal is in fact treated as a nuclear zone and as such has an ORSEC-RAD plan (*Organisation des Secours, Radioactivité*) in case of accident. But in theory the plan is secret, and the decision to activate it rests with the prefectoral authorities (i.e., at *département* level). Although regionally the Arsenal forms the object of numerous academic studies, this has always been on account of its place within the working-class movement and its influence on local politics. They never go into the nuclear aspect, whether from the point of view of risk or from that of pollution.

Flamanville power station was built at a time when the French public was beginning to become aware of the risk represented by civil nuclear power. The years 1975–80 saw the heyday of demonstrations at the sites of nuclear power stations all over France. At Flamanville the majority of the farmers and fishermen of the municipality, together with a few second home owners, spurred on and supported by militant members of the environmental movement (most of them teachers in the region), fought a fierce campaign against the construc-tion of the power station.[8] On the other hand the tradespeople, the local councillors, and the working population made up of former miners tended to be for it. A referendum was held in the municipality, and a majority voted in favour. From then on, further struggle was futile.

Today the nuclear power station is in full operation, and if the quarrels provoked by its construction have died down, traces of them nevertheless remain in terms of local political loyalties. These loyalties in fact regrouped when it came to protesting against the proposed route of the high-tension line. Despite a vigorous campaign by environmentalists and elected representatives, the municipalities affected were unable to get the cables buried or even shifted. Their one victory concerned a school complex that lay in one of the power-line corridors; they managed to make EDF rebuild it some distance away.

So the cables carrying electricity away from the nuclear power station swoop rhythmically along a double line of pylons ranged every 500 metres from Flamanville to the reprocessing plant by way of the Tollevast dispersal station on the southern outskirts of Cherbourg. The landscape of la Hague is thus crowned with a forest of spindly trees like giant dried cow-parsley heads sticking up from every ridge, providing a metallic vegetation to match the slabs of concrete, soaring corkscrew chimneys, and swivelling cranes of the industrial complex that dominates the moor.

The reprocessing plant aroused little opposition when building began in 1962. The story that the people of la Hague have to tell of the dawn of the nuclear age in this place has the ring of a veritable saga, with the same episodes recounted repeatedly in tones of mingled realism and humour that convey a particular vision of the world as seen through the eyes of those who lived through this period.

It started with the appearance on the moor of surveyors who said little and did not stand on ceremony:

> Well, it began back around 1954–5. We used to see them walking about the place. Never asked any questions . . . Used to fire off a sort of shell to find out the hardness of the ground. Measured the wind as well . . . One day they arrived with the first drilling gadget and tried to set it up in a field belonging to old mother G. She slung them out. Quite right, too, basically. They just turned up like travellers . . . Invaders, if you like! When you asked them what they were doing, they'd say any old thing. One time it was building a plastics factory, another time a fertiliser plant, or else it was a factory to make saucepans, aluminium engines, you name it . . .

The project was then announced to the elected representatives of the region. Here is the account given by the man who was *conseiller général* (the local member of the general council of the *département*) at the time:

> Then one day we heard officially. I had a letter from the prefect inviting me to attend a meeting to be held at the prefecture in Saint-Lô [the capital of Manche *département*]. I remember arriving at the prefecture at the same time as Mr Schmidt, a member of parliament for the department, and us saying to each other: 'What are they going to tell us now?' We went into the prefect's office, and there were three people to announce the news: an ex-minister, Mr Galley, who was there on behalf of the CEA, a Mr Duboz, an engineer, who was to build the plant, and Mr Jaigu, a humanities

teacher seconded to the CEA. Then Mr Galley told us they were going to build an atomic plant on the moorland of la Hague. The mayor of Cherbourg was there, too, and lots of other people as well . . . It was like it always is with every government, they act as if they own the place, as if they can do anything, that's all they think about . . . I told them: 'I'm just a farmer, myself, so I can't speak from the scientific point of view . . . But have you thought of notifying the mayors of the municipalities concerned?' No, they said. Well, isn't it about time you did? That'll look good, won't it, the press'll be coming out with the news in the morning . . . The mayors will have to be seen this evening.'

That was when the mayors received their nocturnal summons. A few hours after the meeting in the prefect's office a police van set off along the sunken lanes of la Hague to call on all the mayors of the canton and hand them their orders to attend a meeting at Beaumont-Hague town hall at nine o'clock that very evening. There they found the secretary-general of the prefecture waiting for them, accompanied by the *conseiller général* who told them that it had been decided in high places to build a factory on the la Hague promontory to manufacture plutonium for military purposes, using uranium. 'Nobody asked any questions, nobody gave his opinion, because we hadn't been asked for any authorisation. Anyway, by the time they told us, the newspaper was already printed with the news in it.'

Then came the period of negotiations and of the local farmers' wily attempts to sell their moorland for the highest price possible. But the landowners went into battle in broken order, making the seige-layers' task that much easier. The stretch of countryside that the CEA wanted for the plant comprised a very large number of plots belonging to nearly 300 proprietors, some of whom had long since left la Hague and showed little attachment to land that had never brought them in much money.

> There was some attempt to form a defence committee, but the CEA people went to see the owners who no longer lived in la Hague, particularly those who had the poorest land. When the owner saw he stood to get a good price for what was worthless land, he sold straight away. Afterwards the CEA people came back and said: 'Well, we've got that bit, he's sold up.' So they sold up, too. What did you expect them to do? Oh, the money was good: 'One and a half cows' [*une vaque et demin*], when it wasn't worth a half.

In Normandy the milch cow is the measure of everything.

That left the problem of the farmers whose farms had become too small after these massive land purchases: 'That's all very well, you take away our land, but there'll be less of it for us to work. So then they said: "If you like we'll earmark jobs for you." That's how people went to work at the plant. There are half a dozen of us in the same boat.'

This policy of paying a high price for the land and in some instances offering immediate work that was better paid than most jobs available locally silenced all desire to protest. At no time did the CEA resort to compulsory purchase orders. Less than two years after the first discussions, construction of the plant was under way.

Then came the period of rumours regarding the safety of such an establishment. In an attempt to scotch them, the *conseiller général* suggested to the CEA that they invite the local elected representatives to visit Marcoule, where a plant of the type planned for la Hague had been in operation for some time. The episode of the 'trip to Marcoule' will remain etched on their memories for ever.

> People were saying so many silly things around here . . . that women were having children with two heads, calves too, everything was deformed, that there were seven kilometers around Marcoule that were out of bounds . . . So I went to Paris specially to tell them: 'Listen, I think it would change everything if you agreed to let us visit the place and meet and talk to the people there by ourselves.' That's what they did. We flew down there and had a pretty good time, actually – doesn't all have to be doom and gloom. There were nineteen mayors and deputy mayors in the party, and we also had the chairman of the dairy co-operative and a representative of the Beaumont tradesmen with us. It was in December, lovely weather. At Marcoule the first person we saw was the mayor of Bagnols-sur-Cèze, a very talkative fellow who made a long speech about the damage they had suffered down there during the war . . . After that the mayors of the three municipalities in which the plant is situated all spoke, then off we went to lunch in a château . . . In the afternoon we saw over the plant . . . Next day we were shown round the co-operative wine cellars. Everywhere we went we asked if it was all true, what people said . . . And every time the answer came back that there was nothing in it . . . We spent the evening in Marseille eating their special fish soup, then caught the train home via Saclay. Oh, we had a good time, all right, and there were those who took advantage . . .
>
> The rumours persisted, you can't stop people talking, but it was different for us now because we were able to tell people that what they were saying was not true, we'd seen the place. You'll always get folk who think they know better, though.

Next it was the turn of the parish priests of la Hague to make the trip to Marcoule in order to assess the impact of such an establishment on religious life. They too came back convinced, because as one old lady remembered who lived in one of the municipalities on whose land the plant was to be built: 'The priest told us we shouldn't be afraid of progress and said that maybe, in twenty years' time, there would be a city with its own cathedral up on the moor at Jobourg.'

At that time, in this rural society, the priest's opinion was listened to and followed. The pro-nuclear stance adopted by the clergy weighed heavily in the Hagars' passive acceptance of the reprocessing plant: 'It was the priests who let the atom in. Reverend D. was one who gave lectures after visiting Marcoule, saying that the atom equalled salvation.'[9]

Notables, clergy, landowners, they all or nearly all swallowed the idea that the plant must be allowed to become established on the moor, or at least that it was futile to oppose it. So much so, in fact, that in this account of the early days of that great adventure, when the modern world burst in on their remote peninsula, one gains an impression, among the men and women of la Hague, of a certain pride at having managed to take up the challenge that the late twentieth century had hurled at their feet.

> I'm not scared of the plant ... It's dangerous, I grant you, but what isn't dangerous nowadays? When they laid on electricity to the farms fifty years back people said: 'You put electricity in the cowsheds and it'll set fire to everything.' Our grandparents didn't want the railway. You can't go backwards. You've got to move with the times.

Pride, yes, but with an admixture of fatalism. The plant was imposed on them with no public consultation and no real democratic debate. How, in such circumstances, could plans decided elsewhere be opposed? In any case, the people of la Hague are not in the habit of making a show of their opinions. They do not discuss things, particularly not with outsiders (*horsains*)[10] and most emphatically not with 'Parisians'. And how do you argue with technicians who come along to explain complex industrial projects? What do you say to civil servants who present fat planning files? It is at such times as these that the silent, doubting nature of the Hagar asserts itself with the resigned comment: 'Just got to trust them, haven't you? They're the ones that know!'

Granted, a few farmers, a few fishermen, a few craft tradesmen, and a few local councillors did, right from the beginning, dare to state their opposition to and distrust of the plans put forward by the CEA:

> At the outset we were the only ones who resisted the construction of the plant (recall one couple who used to work in local government). We were against it right from the start. It's a well-known fact that they took the mayors round everywhere ... The prefects came and met the municipal councils, telling them: 'You'll have splendid jobs, there'll be plenty of work, business will thrive ... and on top of that there's no danger at all ... I'm relying on you to tell people that.' Then it was a swift handshake all round and they were off again. People aren't inquisitive round here, they didn't ask questions, so it just happened automatically, the only argument in favour being 'money'. That was enough ... Above all, people were so certain that the whole thing had been fixed in advance, that it was no use protesting or filling in the survey forms because it had all been decided over their heads. So yes, you can certainly say there's no opposition here!

This sort of outlook and this way of going about things explain why the anti-nuclear protest has never had a very high profile at la Hague. Moreover, in the heyday of the anti-nuclear campaign, between 1976 and 1981 when the plant was being extended and above all when the first ships loaded with foreign spent fuel for reprocessing docked at Cherbourg, the driving forces of protest came mainly from outside the canton. At la Hague itself there was not, at this period, any general discussion of these matters among municipal councillors, despite the fact that they had been brought together in a specially formed assembly serving the new district local authority. Admittedly, the extension was entirely contained within the boundaries of the land already purchased by the CEA, so that the people of the canton were not required to pronounce on it. As for all the facilities required for building the extension or maintaining the existing plant, this was negotiated by COGEMA's *Grand chantier* superintendent who called on the mayor of each municipality individually, doing deals: municipal infrastructure in return for residential zoning, a road diversion in return for a modular housing development, jobs at the plant in return for an industrial estate. The great saga of the modern world ends up as a funny story!

Let me just add, to give some idea of the blend of muttered irony and timid discontent that forms the prevailing mood on the peninsula today, that there are those who say: 'There are eight anti-nuclear people left at la Hague.'

Those eight protestors are known, and each has his or her own particular character, way of going about things, and role within the protest movement. But if they are occasionally treated with contempt, people who never protest themselves will tell you in no uncertain terms: 'We've got to hang on to them. They're our guarantee of safety.'

That assertion provides a glimpse of the repressed anxiety present in those who lacked either the ability or the know-how to oppose this formidable undertaking that has invaded their moor, drastically altering its landscape and destroying their identity. The handful of determined protestors who have led an underground resistance movement right from the start, a radical struggle, doomed in advance, against an all-powerful bureaucratic machine, represent the only outlet, in the minds of those whose children will occasionally accuse them of having 'sold la Hague', for the mistrust that these men and women are unwilling or unable to voice openly. That outlet must not be sealed; those mouths must never be closed.

However, the people of la Hague do have other, more surreptitious ways of giving expression to their fears or their guilty consciences, namely in the polling booth at election time, in rumour (that other mouth that never stops talking), and in certain subconscious activities enabling them to hold the nuclear order that has been imposed on them at a distance. I shall be examining all these defences in subsequent chapters.

Marked places, marked objects

The reason why it was possible for these various industrial establishments to be built without obvious opposition on this rocky promontory lashed by the fury of the seas is that in a sense their places had been marked out in advance.

The Arsenal, built nearly 200 years ago, forms an integral part of Cherbourg. It has helped to shape its history, imparting a certain flavour to the town, an air of originality that distinguishes it from other towns in Normandy. For the people of Cherbourg, what matters is that the Arsenal should go on being there, beside the harbour, sheltered within its great jetty. So what if the workshops have been taken over by nuclear power!

The power station nestling in the Flamanville cliffs occupies the precise site of the old undersea iron mines, and ex-miners who now work at the power station still say: 'I'm off down the mine.' For them, nothing has changed.

As for the people of la Hague, if they have allowed their moor to be swallowed up by a high-risk industry, it is because since time immemorial they have always looked towards the sea, had their eye on distant horizons, and devoted all their attention to defending their shoreline against human conquest. The symbolic world of the Hagars, their collective memory, and their imaginations are stamped through and through by the proximity of these coasts, which even today remain in their natural state. The folk of la Hague patrol these wild, inhospitable shores incessantly, exploit them shamelessly, and people them with all their dreams. Indeed, it is these uncultivated beaches that form the true communal spaces of these topographically scattered hamlets that have no squares, no streets in which people may gather, and where each household seems cut off from the others, withdrawn into itself, preoccupied with nursing its privacy behind windowless gable-ends. As a result, these strips between land and sea have come to fill the role of commons, places where people meet. Here social constraints are swept aside and all the legendary potential of the region is concentrated. The shore is the haunt of fairies and wizards, the domain of saints and demons. Here the peninsula's principal marked spots are located, and this is the setting of most of the events in the tales and legends that are still recounted today. The limits of the peninsula are marked by two caves. The *trou Balignan* is or rather was an opening in the Flamanville cliffs, said to have been home to a monstrous serpent that repeatedly laid waste to the region. The monster was turned to stone by a look from St Germain, who suddenly appeared floating on the sea, borne up by a cartwheel. The cave on the other side, on the east coast, is named after St Colombe, a young martyr who met her death at that spot. Between the monster and the saint guarding the gateways of their homeland, the old Hagars dotted their coastline with 'fairy gardens', 'magician's caves', and 'witches' rocks' as well as identifying the abyss into which the White Lady hurled the lone traveller who had unwisely made a habit of following her on foggy nights. The pendant of all this was that the attraction exerted by the shore and its resources and the lure of all that hailed from the sea, from afar, from beyond the familiar horizon, was a rejection of the rest of the territory or at the very least a certain indifference to the fate of its cultivated fields and reclaimed moorland. If the people of la Hague accepted the nuclear reprocessing plant easily, it was doubtless because it was erected on land they had always regarded as remote and somehow foreign. That strangers should come along and appropriate that land in the service of their own technology was written in the Hagars' destiny. Already during the war the Germans had occupied the place, erecting blockhouses and installing a radar observation station. And today old people will say that 'there's always been a factory' on the moor, while others mutter: 'The invaders are back.'

Each of these three establishments, then, had its place symbolically marked out in the landscape. Now man's imagination has seized on them, attributing relative degrees of danger or harmlessness to each one. Everybody finds his own more reliable than his neighbour's. At Flamanville they are glad they live near the power station because it is far 'cleaner' than the 'dustbin' that has been erected on the moor. In the hamlets up on the moor, people take comfort from being at some distance from the power station, so much more 'dangerous' than their reprocessing plant.

2 The nuclear setting

'The dustbin'! Making a mental note of this derogatory name for the reprocessing plant, let us try to trace the history of it. We shall discover, as we do so, the role and power of words in this place where people tend to use as few of them as possible.

A name usurped

In the beginning there was the CEA and a so-called 'atomic plant'. That, at least, is how the site is referred to on old maps of the region. To the workers and to the people of la Hague it was 'the Jobourg plant' (*l'usine de Jobourg*), from the name of one of the municipalities on whose territory the first workshops were erected.

Along came COGEMA, and from then on the establishment was known as the 'la Hague reprocessing plant' (*usine de retraitement de la Hague*). It is under this title, both technical and geographical, that it appears in the company's organisation chart and is marked on current maps of the region. In official publications, whether scientific or journalistic, the name is shortened to the 'la Hague plant' (*l'usine de la Hague*), and it is under this simplified version of the name that the establishment has achieved its present notoriety. Most French people now believe that 'la Hague' denotes a nuclear plant, unaware that it is actually the name of a region. If you say to someone: 'I'm off to la Hague' (*Je pars à la Hague*), they immediately assume that you are going to visit the plant. To make your meaning clear and at the same time demonstrate that you are a 'local', you have to steer a clever course between your prepositions and say: 'Je vais dans la Hague'.

'People don't realise any more that la Hague is a place,' one inhabitant remarked, not without a trace of bitterness. What is worse, nowadays the name conveys a strongly negative image. Indeed, alongside this onomastic substitution we find a shift in the way in which the fuel reprocessed at the plant is described.

At the beginning it was a question of 'spent nuclear fuel' and of a plant that manufactured plutonium for military purposes. For the people of la Hague, working for the armed forces is part of a familiar tradition in an area where the biggest employer is the Cherbourg

Arsenal. At the time, reaction to the fact that such a plant was being set up on the moor was very positive.

With the extension of reprocessing and the construction of the stockpiling centre, the emphasis switched to the quantities and origin of the spent fuel rods and the productive capacity of the plant in terms of reprocessing. There was little further mention of the precious plutonium, which in fact no one knows what to do with nowadays.[1] Following privatisation of the plant, no more was said about military uses; all the talk was of reprocessing and stockpiling spent fuel. The prestigious image of an establishment devoted to the maintenance of world peace gradually faded, leaving what is no more than a plant for recycling used materials. What made this even harder to accept was the fact that those used materials, like the plant itself, were to come to be viewed with ever-increasing disparagment. Saying or writing 'Spent fuel reprocessing plant' (*Usine de retraitement des combustibles irradiés*) was in fact so cumbersome that at COGEMA and in all the publications they stopped talking about spent fuel rods altogether and spoke only of the reprocessing of nuclear *déchets* and of the stockpiling of *résidues* at ANDRA. Both terms (covered by the English 'waste'; Tr.) are associated in the popular mind with notions of filth, pollution, contagion, and the like.

Then the first consignments of spent fuel arrived from abroad, triggering the first large-scale anti-nuclear demonstrations. In a striking instance of compression, the environmentalists hit on a nickname for the plant that was swiftly taken up by the press and even by scientists: they called it 'the dustbin'. Soon everyone began to think of la Hague as 'the world's atomic dustbin' (*la poubelle atomique du monde*).

The people of la Hague themselves rarely use so derogatory a term to refer to the industrial complex on the moor. They talk about 'the plant' (*usine*), without further qualification, but most often they avoid naming it and say simply 'up there' (*là-haut*), 'the thing' (*la chose*), or 'it' (*ça*), all turns of speech that, one feels, imply a desire to place the object spoken of at a certain distance. The pride that they were able to feel in the early days at seeing such an establishment built in their part of the world is gradually being eclipsed by their growing awareness of the role played by that establishment in the cycle of nuclear energy.

This plant that has invaded their moor, this place where, they are told, a pioneering technology is being developed, is thus seen by others (people who talk about the plant but do not live at la Hague) as a dangerous dump where all the countries of the world may come and empty their nuclear 'dustbins'. And that dump bears the name of their *pays*, their home. How shall a person go on saying that he or she is from la Hague when there is a risk of folk from Caen or Rouen saying in reply, as if la Hague were simply one giant industrial complex: 'All right to shake you by the hand? Not radioactive, are you?'

How, in the circumstances, can anyone be expected to vaunt the quality of the local produce, for example? In fact, to guard against any tendency for the public to reject produce originating from the peninsula, the dairy farmers have removed the name of la Hague from the labels of their milk products, and at auctions and on their stalls the fishermen no longer announce the provenance of their fish or shellfish.

The way in which the plant has taken over the name of the *pays* has upset a whole range of age-old landmarks: 'It [the plant] has stolen everything from us, even our name, even our identity.'

Understandably, then, so far as the people of la Hague are concerned the plant has become 'it', a place with no name, a place they even, in all sorts of ways, try not to see.

A local blind spot

'You can't see the plant from my place ... So we're all right,' I was assured by one resident of a hamlet lying a few hundred metres from the plant as the crow flies. Coming out of his house, however, I had only to look round the back to behold the vast presence of the establishment that has grown up at the bottom of his garden. I came across this kind of selective blindness time and time again. It is as if in these hamlets dotted over the plateau, the only inhabited points from which the reprocessing plant is visible, people have decided not to see it, using a fold in the ground, the way a garden faces, or the position of a housefront to eclipse this untidy, deeply disturbing section of the landscape from view. When the lie of the land is unhelpful, they use the wind: 'Here, if it ever did go up, the wind is often from the west, so I'm not worried myself ... If you live on the other side, you can't be so sure that you ...'

In other words, what the hell! Thanks to either meteorology or topography, these near neighbours of *le nucléaire* feel sheltered or at least like to think they are. Elsewhere, in the tiny villages tucked in the valleys, the land acts as a protective screen and people have no need to adjust the geography in order to be able to say: 'You can't see the plant from here ... so it doesn't bother me. Look, you can see the tower of Auderville church ... You can see the lighthouse ... But you can't see the plant. You can't see anything from here.'

So one way of defending yourself against the invasion of the reprocessing plant with its ever more numerous buildings (and no doubt against the fear that they inspire) is to decide not to see them. In some places this is not hard to do. In others, the landscape needs a little rearranging, but the mechanism is the same, namely denying the existence of the danger by refusing to see its architectural embodiment.

Moreover, Hagars are happy to stress, for the benefit of anyone who asks them whether the plant has not rather blighted their landscape, that this is not so at all: 'You can walk anywhere in la Hague and not see a thing. You can be quite close to it, but the plant's still hidden, you see the sea and the shore, that's all.'

Indeed, for these people the landscape with which they identify and where, as we have seen, their collective memory is situated and many of their social relations occur, is the shore, where land and sea are wed. On this peninsula with its very variegated coastline, where the lie of the land and the constitution of the rock have wrought an infinity of shapes, the Hagars' best-loved landscapes are marine: 'My favourite is St. Martin's Cove when the sun is going down over the sea' . . . 'Jobourg Bill, you have the cliffs and the sea, which is a lovely colour there' . . . 'That's the loveliest spot on la Hague there, Ecalgrain Bay.'

So long as the reprocessing plant does not encroach too much (though it has begun to do so in the case of the Cove of les Moulinets, directly below the plant) on these border territories between land and sea, the people of la Hague will find a way of forgetting its existence and banishing their fears.

The guided tour as exorcism

This trick of rejecting the reality of the plant by intercalating a topographical screen in no way prevents the people of la Hague from manifesting a desire, even a keen desire, to know what goes on 'up there'.

A small group of implacable opponents have decided once and for all they they 'would never set foot in the place', and there are one or two very old and timid folk whose horizon is still bounded by the village street, people who want to have nothing to do with the bustle of the world, who will neither listen to the radio nor watch television, and who elicit the remark: 'For those oldsters, nuclear power is like the next world'. Apart from these few, however, the remaining inhabitants of la Hague have all visited the plant at least once, some of them several times.

Group visits are organised by various associations (there is not a single old people's club that has not had its guided tour) or by constituent bodies, municipal or regional elected representatives, mayors, or *conseillers généraux*. Moreover, these monuments to modern technology, these establishments in which man tames that controversial giant, nuclear energy, which may occasionally turn against him to the point of actually destroying him, do not draw only the people of la Hague. People come from all over France, indeed from all over the world, to visit the reprocessing plant or see over Flamanville power station. Nowadays they are as popular as that other local monument, Mont-Saint-Michel. Indeed, they are on the same tourist circuit. For Hagars, though, there is something more involved than a fascination with the achievements of the modern age: they need to know what goes on at the installation that is perpetually spawning new buildings up on the moor. In addition to the spell cast by these premises that are in part open to inspection and in part out of bounds (because of course visitors are never shown everything), in part high above ground, in part below (some workshops rise to twenty-seven metres above the moor and extend as far beneath it), there is the need to draw reassurance from hearing someone say that all precautions are taken and there is nothing to fear. These aspects emerge clearly from the thoughts of this Goury restaurateur: 'I've been round the plant two or three times ... in fact, I ought to go back for a bit of a refresher course. It's ages since I was there last. But, you know, once you get to understand what they're doing up there ... Well, you feel easier in your mind ...'

The guided tours combine sound and vision in such a way as to give an impression of immense reliability. Seeing those tanks of blue water with the baskets of uranium rods bathing in their limpid depths, noting the massive earthquake-proof columns on which they rest, being able to touch the steel fins of the mighty containers used to transport the nuclear fuel as they stand in neat ranks in their storage area, or being invited to view the films glorifying the meticulous operations of white-coated men – all these things generate among visitors that feeling of confidence that flows from what is visible and tangible.

This glimpse of reality that visitors are given during the guided tour, coupled with the so manifestly positive explanations provided on the very premises where the nuclear transformation takes place, has the effect of calming people. In any case, how is the visitor to argue with the facts and figures supplied in such profusion by a succession of self-assured, reassuring speakers? He or she can only nod and look suitably reassured. 'People don't know what to say or what to ask,' one lecturer at the la Hague plant told me. 'After the film [on reprocessing] they don't usually have any questions.' But in any case the visit is timed to the minute and leaves little time for a discussion to get under way.

Their serenity thus restored, Hagars find it easier to forget about the plant, put it at a distance, and believe themselves safe.

Whether they are pushing the plant away in their minds or getting close to it on a guided tour, their actions serve the same purpose of trying to forget a haunting presence. With the same end in view, there are many other possible tactics that the people who live in the hamlets employ as the mood or their make-up takes them.

Some feign indifference: 'The plant ... Oh, I don't give a damn! We've all got to die, what does it matter whether from that or something else!'

Others opt for a fatalism tinged with irony: 'No one's safe any more nowadays. We saw that with the cloud from Chernobyl ... So we'll die first, that's all!'

Others again just do not want to know, denying that there is any danger and placing their faith in the experts: 'They know what they're doing up there! I trust the scientists, myself, they know better than us what they're talking about.'

And then there are those who seize on the invisibility of radio-activity: 'If there were any contamination, you'd see it ... But the grass and trees around the plant are as green and vigorous as anywhere else.'

Or they will point to all the other kinds of pollution that threaten the environment and that nobody seems to care about. The fishermen moan more about the oil that messes up their nets ('That's a much bigger threat') or the over-fishing indulged in by *horsains*, which is exhausting fish stocks. Hunters who patrol the moor around the plant accuse the farmers of using pesticides that are destroying the game: 'They're the worst polluters ...'

As for the farmers, they say they are more worried about the traffic on the roads (moving stock from one field to another is now a major undertaking, they complain) or about rising land prices than about radioactive contamination of their pasturage: 'Anyway, they keep an eye on it, and if there was anything there they'd tell us ...'

A few – but only a few – will admit to being afraid of the proximity of the plant, like the young local-government officer in Beaumont who asked for a transfer 'because she couldn't stand being so close' or the farmer's wife who confessed: 'Since that's been there on the plateau, right outside my house, I've not felt alive any more [*je ne vis plus*]. But when you have land here, when you've bought a place here, what are you supposed to do? You stay ...'

The remaining inhabitants have found a way of silencing their fears in the far from negligible economic repercussions of the advent of the nuclear industry. Remarks like this are commonplace: 'The plant has meant jobs for the local lads. If it closed, there'd be major unemployment' ... 'The plant saved the place from becoming depopulated' ... 'Without the plant, la Hague would have been doomed.'

But has not la Hague doomed itself, in a way, by accepting the financial manna spread about by these industrial installations?

The gold mine of the *Grand chantier*

It all began with the construction of the original plant in 1962. At that time there was very little upheaval. The CEA's land purchases had, as we have seen, proceeded with no opposition to speak of, and the plant was largely built by local firms using labour recruited locally, around Cherbourg or at Flamanville (the Diélette mine near Flamanville had just closed, releasing a substantial workforce). To accommodate the technicians to come, just two low-cost housing projects were built, one in the suburbs of Cherbourg and the other in the centre of Beaumont, the cantonal capital. To give the atomic age upon which the region was embarked a suitably splendid inauguration, someone had the idea of making the new housing development look like an atom surrounded by its electrons, as if the first stone of the city of the future had been laid there.

The founders' plans failed to have quite the impact expected, because in 1976 most of the flats in 'atom city' stood empty. Around that time EDF decided to abandon the graphite gas-cooled reactors for which the reprocessing plant had been designed. The establishment was left ticking over, and a certain number of employees, encouraged by attractive bonuses, took jobs elsewhere. There were rumours that the plant was about to close. The beacon of the modern world built on this windswept plateau had, it seemed, been no more than a stubble fire.

In 1976, however, it all started again. The CEA's decision to open the High-Level Oxide (HAO) workshops at la Hague, which were capable of reprocessing spent fuel from pressurised-water reactors, followed by the takeover of the establishment by COGEMA, resurrected the golden opportunities represented by a major construction project.

The changes assumed substantial proportions with the start of work on Flamanville power station, which was spread over the period 1978 to 1981, then with the opening of the vast building site (the *Grand chantier*) made necessary by the construction of UP3 and the extension of UP2 (see map, p. 74). Not only the area surrounding the site itself, nor even just the canton, but the entire *département* of la Manche got carried away in a mad transformation, the effects of which extended to every aspect of individual and collective existence, social as well as economic, disrupting everything down to the wooded landscape bequeathed to la Hague by the working practices of nineteenth-century graziers.

It is important for us to realise that not only the purpose but also the sheer scale of these operations represented a complete break with the life forces of the locality, both occupational and demographic. These enormously complex nuclear construction sites are run by specialist civil-engineering firms of a kind that simply did not exist locally; they had to be brought in from outside, which meant that settlement areas had to be provided for them. Such firms have their own workforce and draw only to a very limited extent on the local population. Consequently, a whole 'off-site' infrastructure of roads, road transport, industrial estates, housing of all kinds, and educational, sports, and cultural facilities became essential in order to receive the 320 or so companies with their 7,000 employees (including their families, some 15,000 people in all) required by what was to become the biggest building site in Europe, total investment in which over the space of ten years came to fifty billion francs (£5 billion). Given the size of these figures, one can appreciate that the region has been hit by a veritable shock wave that has shredded the old social fabric, transformed the traditional economy, and upset every kind of local demographic and political equilibrium. In this colossal upheaval the municipalities of la Hague have of course not gone unscathed.

To take care of the off-site arrangements, a special *Grand chantier* procedure was decided upon in 1979 under the direction of an 'Inter-ministerial Area Planning Committee'. The role of this committee was to co-ordinate road-building programmes and provide sufficient social and educational facilities and new housing to receive and integrate the incoming workforce. A co-ordinator ensured collaboration between the local communities and the body responsible for the *Grand chantier*, known as the 'New Techniques Company' (*Société des Techniques nouvelles*; it used to be called *Saint-Gobain nucléaire* and is still referred to as SGN), which COGEMA appointed to manage the project.

This procedure made it possible to define in advance as well as co-ordinate and provide for the needs of the companies and their workers in terms of accommodation, transport, schools, and so on. In all these areas, things went off without any major problems. Granted, there were waiting lists for permanent housing, the road infra-structure took rather longer to materialise than had been envisaged, and in the early years of the project la Hague threatened to founder under the effects of new roads being cut through, buildings erected all over the place, quarries opened up in a totally unplanned fashion, country lanes dug up to make way for mains drainage, and so on. But by and large la Hague escaped the almost apocalyptic situations that have been described in connection with other projects of this kind.[2] In fact, now that the project is entering upon its final phase the head of SGN is already claiming victory:

Into a region numbering one hundred and thirty thousand inhabitants we have unloaded a further fifteen thousand . . . All the infrastructure has been created on time and on a sufficient scale. There has been no housing crisis, even if rents have gone up, no rogue, off-site operations, no unauthorised caravan parks . . . This site has always maintained a low profile.[3]

Let us take a look from outside and see what actually happened.

To start with, it is perhaps regrettable that, at the level of the vast region affected by the *Grand chantier*,[4] it never occurred to the elected representatives to create an institution that would have taken an overall view of the necessary development work and where it should be sited. The *département* of la Manche, the town of Cherbourg, and the suburban municipalities all acted in isolation, purely on their own account. As for la Hague canton, where the municipalities had regrouped to form a district, it played no direct part, at either the initial or development stages, in planning the various installations called for by an industrial undertaking of this kind. Each municipality made decisions on its own account, with the co-ordinator going from door to door (that is to say, from town hall to town hall) trading pre-financed housing to accommodate construction-site workers or COGEMA employees against sports facilities or schools, roads or harbours, against a waste-water purification programme, and so on. At the end of all this wheeling and dealing, nine municipalities out of nineteen agreed to become 'reception municipalities' (*communes d'accueil*).

The ones that turned the procedure down did not escape the changes. Large numbers of detached houses were built on their land, and private developers took the place of communal initiatives. Also, in every town and village a special programme run by COGEMA enabled property-owners to restore traditional housing for rent to executive staff. Management personnel tend to live on private housing estates, while the workers live in caravans or in modular developments. As a result, virtually all the municipalities of the canton have seen their populations increase. To keep pace with this growth and integrate the newcomers it was necessary to open new schools or reopen old ones, increase the number of classes, take on extra council workers, provide leisure areas and sports facilities, lay on water, and put in various kinds of drainage. All or nearly all the municipalities threw themselves into major public works, taking advantage of the money that came to them as their share of the taxes paid by COGEMA and the companies involved in the *Grand chantier*. Virtually every village now boasts its own hall and sports ground, while the back lanes have all been metalled and the village streets lined with pavements.

The problem, however, remains as to what will become of these dwellings and these facilities when building work at the plant reaches completion. The vision of the empty flats of Beaumont's 'atom city' still haunts the memories of the mayors of the canton. Some feel they have done better than their neighbours:

> I can tell you, there are some municipalities where I wouldn't care to be mayor ... In Beaumont they had that already after the construction of la Hague, plan A. They were full up and then from one day to the next there was nobody, the people had all left to work elsewhere or had quit to go to Cherbourg ... I'll be all right here [Urville/Nacqueville]. When all the housing reverts to the municipality, I'll still be able to let it. We're well placed here, out of town but not too far, it's the ideal spot ... The countryside ... And you've got the seaside too ... People are going to want to live here rather than anywhere else ...

Others are more pessimistic. They worry about the future:

> So far as the life of the village is concerned, opting for the housing estate was a positive move. For one thing, we've had specific loans to put in council facilities, and that has also made it possible for us to open a second class this year and even offer school meals. It's put a bit of life in the place, you know? But one wonders what will happen when the population starts to fall off. All of a sudden we've got young people with children of primary-school age, but in five or six years there'll be no more births and no more new building ... For the time being, all right, it's an improvement, but is it going to last in the long term?

A joint so-called 'post-*Grand chantier*' association was set up in 1987 to look into and suggest solutions to the problem of sustaining economic activity and high population levels in the region once the building work is completed.

It is particularly in the nine 'reception municipalities', where building and infrastructure operations have assumed vast proportions, that these questions present themselves in an acute form. There a number of private housing developments (some 300 dwellings altogether) have been built on a larger or smaller scale, depending on the location. Urville-Nacqueville has virtually an entire village comprising some 145 houses, while Jobourg opted for a modest estate of ten detached houses. Apart from one or two instances, where an attempt has been made to echo the local vernacular architecture, most of these developments exhibit the distressing monotony of design typical of most modern private housing in France. Sited on the outskirts of municipalities, they form as it were satellite hamlets. It is the traditional pattern of settlement in this scattered habitat, but it is hardly conducive to integrating in the life of the village newcomers who first have to learn the ways of this austere land.

The permanent housing stock is insufficient to accommodate all the site workers, for such sites bring with them a whole population of nomadic workers who, together with their families, move in a fleet of caravans from one location to another, following their employers. Moorings had to be found for them, too. Three pieces of land capable of taking 150 caravans were duly set aside, but these were soon seen to be inadequate as caravans began to overflow from the official sites and settle on private land, usually rented from farmers. The result is that the countryside is now littered with the camps of these twentieth-century nomads, set up behind hedges, beneath electricity pylons, in orchards and farmyards, giving an almost 'gold rush' appearance to this part of the Norman landscape.

Those who do not own a caravan and cannot get into permanent accommodation are left with the mobile-home solution, where ranks of temporary dwellings lined up in a field form a kind of modular development centred on a communal facilities block. There are three such developments in and around Beaumont. Two of them, reserved for single men, consist of bungalows housing four tenants apiece and comprising four bedrooms with a shared living-room–cum–kitchen.

The caretaker of one of these mobile-home parks had this to say:

They have a cooking-stove and one fridge between two . . . They're well set up. There are Frenchmen and immigrants, but they all live in groups, there's no mixing. The Muslims make their supper, their tea, taking turns . . . They say their prayers in their bedrooms, where they'll nearly all have a secondhand telly . . .

The other park is for workers living with their families. Here each family is allotted its own mobile home, a wooden shell containing three rooms, a kitchen corner, and another corner that does duty as a bathroom. Family and communal life are difficult in these modular developments, with overcrowding leading to a lack of privacy not just within families but also between families, forced as they are to live on top of one another the whole time. For where can a person go, living in Beaumont without a car? The mobile-home parks, like all the villages, are not served by any form of public transport linking them with Cherbourg except on a Saturday, when COGEMA lays on a coach to take its employees the twelve miles into town in the morning and bring them back in the evening. The women living permanently on these parks, unable to get jobs locally, find their virtual imprisonment hard to bear. Isolated by the fact that their relatives live elsewhere, they also feel rejected by the local community.

The fact is that these temporary estates house most of the foreign workers (mainly Turks, North Africans, and Portuguese) who make up almost a quarter of the total *Grand chantier* workforce, which is to say some 1,500 people at the peak period of development. The different nationalities were first separated ('to avoid any problems between them', I was told), then divided up and parcelled out to various points within the area of influence surrounding the la Hague site: Barneville-Carteret, Tourlaville, Sainte-Mère-Eglise, Cherbourg, Beaumont, and so on. The intention, no doubt, was to keep below the much-talked-about threshold of tolerance, for it is an article of faith among sociologists that above the 10 per cent mark there is a danger of racial conflict between natives and foreigners.

La Hague: an exploded society

So here you have these villages inhabited by new, heterogeneous, mobile populations with whom the old residents attempt to coexist or whom they pretend to ignore. You have these communities of immigrants, most of whom have been in France for fifteen years or more, so have no language problem. Yet the people of la Hague are barely aware of their presence; between them and the aliens, relations are virtually non-existent. All the mayors confirm this with a note of surprise: 'There's no problem with the immigrants ... We don't see them ... They keep themselves to themselves, some communities even policing themselves.'

At la Hague, as in the other towns and villages where they have been grouped together, the immigrants have remained completely cut off from local life. Politely but firmly, they are kept at a distance from the public places where French people gather: a particular restaurant, say, where the proprietor says he refuses to serve immigrants on the pretext that there are no tables free, or the dance halls or fashionable discos where young aliens do not go because they know their presence will not be tolerated. In Beaumont the Turks and the North Africans each have their own cafe, while in Cherbourg they have their place of worship and the Koranic school. In Briquebec and les Pieux they purchase their Mediterranean produce at markets that are well stocked with it nowadays; their meat they buy direct from the abbatoir or from a special butcher. As people delight in pointing out, the immigrants are able to find locally (or not far away, at least) everything they need in order to live 'the way they do at home, without bothering anyone or getting in anyone's way'.

In Cherbourg and Briquebec young immigrants have started their own football team, actually called 'The Young Turks'. In such ways they do indeed keep themselves to themselves, mingling very little with groups of French youths. The number of mixed marriages that have taken place throughout the *département* over the ten-year period during which the construction sites have been in operation can be counted on the fingers of one hand. Instances of cohabitation are slightly more numerous but tend to be unstable and are often frowned upon. Speaking of such mixed couples living together outside marriage, people use the extremely derogatory expression: *Ils font cul commun* ('They're sharing arse').

As for the single men grouped together in the modular developments, they too keep themselves to themselves. On Saturdays the one who owns a car will drive his barrack mates in search of simple pleasures: 'There's no brothel in Cherbourg and no tarts . . . Pimps from Paris will sometimes bring women up in a caravan . . . There's a queue, then!'   So these bachelor immigrants live entirely apart from the local community in an isolation that is stressed as well as symbolised by the wire fences surrounding the mobile-home parks, by the warden watching the entrance twenty-four hours a day, and above all by draconian site regulations, imposed by the corporate landlord, banning all night visits.

Life is probably easier for those immigrants who have come here with their families. Some of them (not many) are even decently housed. For all of them, however, single men and families, those who have been in France for a while and those who have just arrived, there is the dread of tomorrow, when the end of their contract on the works site will mean their having to leave their temporary home and resume the roving search for a fresh contract. From site to site, these immigrants live in utter solitude, perpetually on the fringes of our society.

For the French people newly arrived in the villages, links with the local community are friendlier and more flexible, relationships easier to establish. This is particularly true if they move into one of the detached houses on the new estates or if they build their own. The local council then assumes that they are likely to stay longer than those who take accommodation in the temporary developments. Moreover, those who move into the detached houses often enjoy quite high professional status within COGEMA or one of the associated companies, and this is thought to place them in a good position as regards contacting sources of loans and employment. So the local communities have no hesitation in abandoning their traditional notables and choosing other political bosses from among the newcomers. The incoming populations thus become integrated through their members' joining cultural societies or sports clubs, participating in the political machinery of local life, and chairing the many council committees, for example. In reality, however, though old and new residents may live side by side, they are hardly acquainted and see little of one another.

To understand this, we must picture what life was like at la Hague before these great upheavals.

In these municipalities, topographically fragmented as they are into hamlets or groups of dwellings, there is no traditional place where people may gather to meet together except, as we have seen, the seashore, where in certain circumstances the different age groups (children, adolescents, young people, adults) used to stroll.[5] Only the old would gather each day to sit and chat on the watch seats set up along the shore where, sheltered from the west wind, they commanded a view of the beach and the horizon.

These elements of social rupture were compounded by the marked austerity of local customs, whereby no evening gatherings brought together the members of a hamlet, even in the depths of winter, and no impromptu celebrations broke the wearying, monotonous daily rhythm of life and work. As the year rolled round, a small number of ceremonies – Christmas, Candlemas, and in summer the great co-operative labours in the fields (the *corvées d'honneur* such as haymaking and harvest) – brought the members of the community together. Otherwise, life was hard in the old days, with little room for freedom, particularly for young people, kept under constant surveillance by their elders or by the village priest. Everyone here lived and still does live within a tight group of close relatives, seeing little of others. And anyone not born in the municipality remains forever an outsider, an *horsain*: 'I've been ten years at la Hague now and I don't know anybody,' one shopkeeper exclaimed. 'And I could die fifty years hence and still be a stranger! Oh, they're polite enough, they bid you welcome, but that's as far as it goes!' And a woman in her fifties protested: 'I'm from the next village, but folk here don't look on me as belonging to the village. I've been here thirty years, mind! But no, when I come along they always break off what they were talking about. No one would ever tell me a secret . . . I'm still not one of them.'

The most prominent feature of this Hagar society is thus the lack of integrating elements both in the scattered nature of these municipalities, consisting as they do of groups of dwellings linked by no more than a very sparse network of lanes, and in the forms of sociability, which scarcely favour informal gatherings. It is a society in which the supposedly traditional structures of welcome, usually associated automatically with rural life, hardly exist. Under the impact of depopulation and of people leaving the area to look for work, most kinship networks have broken down, while technological changes in agriculture have done away with the old communal celebrations.

So it was a society turned in upon itself, an egalitarian society, certainly, but one that was also dominated by the old and by its notables that, with the arrival of the plant, suffered the shock of abrupt industrialisation. Understandably, for certain members of the working population with no prospect of finding a job locally, *le nucléaire* appeared to hold out tremendous hope. A Nacqueville man recalls:

> I left school with good technical qualifications in '59, well, no mystery about finding a job then, it was quite straightforward . . . The Arsenal was out, you got in there on a competitive entry exam at fourteen or fifteen . . . Then

there were the Amiot shipyards. Aside from that there was nothing . . .
With a technical diploma of the kind I was able to get at the time, well, you
either went to Caen or you moved to Paris and worked for Renault, Simca,
or Citroën. So when I found out during my military service in '62 that they
were going to build an atomic plant at la Hague, I was a taker straight away
. . . I took my technicians' diploma in electronics, and that's how I got into
the CEA . . .

So the installation of the plant, with the job prospects it offered
(synonymous, particularly for youngsters, with access to financial
independence and freedom), was warmly welcomed by some people,
who set about trying to get work there. From then on a rift gradually
developed at the heart of Hagar society between those who worked at
the plant and those who refused to apply for or failed to obtain
positions there.

In the early days, when operations on the site required few skills,
large numbers of local workers were recruited. Farmers whose land
had been taken or who had no further wish to go on farming,
craft-tradesmen, or people who worked for local businesses, attracted
by high wages and stability of employment, joined the plant as
guards, decontaminators, or HGV drivers. Their children were able to
stay on at school and continue in further education and were then in
turn taken on by COGEMA, citing the 'family' clause of the collective
agreement, which commits the company, where two applicants are
equally qualified, to giving the job to the one who has a close relative
already working at the plant. In addition to this clause, COGEMA has
developed a local employment programme in agreement with the
elected representatives and the unions that sets out to give priority to
local job applicants, subject to their level of training and the requirements of the plant. Apart from the fact that this kind of family
recruitment policy is by no means easy to implement in reality (the
training of allegedly 'related' applicants is often inappropriate, and
above all the definition of the term 'local' can vary enormously,
depending on one's point of view),[6] it also gives the world of the
COGEMA workforce an ambivalent image, prompting extreme and
contradictory interpretations that exacerbate the divisions within this
society.

There are those who see the plant as a closed world entered only by
members of certain chosen kindreds: 'COGEMA is like the Arsenal,
they take you on from father to son . . . It's nepotism.' Others take a
different view, like this young trainee employed by one of the
subcontractors: 'COGEMA's a family business. My father, my aunt,
my cousin, and my brother all work there . . . So I'm trying to get in,
too.'

However, when questions are asked about the pollution caused by the plant and the fears to which it gives rise, they will all admit, with similar abruptness: 'You can't want to be in it and knock it at the same time.'

Criticising *le nucléaire*, in other words, is tantamount to jeopardising your own and your family's source of employment. In fact, some people see this policy of recruiting by families as a deliberate move on the part of the plant management: 'Here in la Hague there's not a single family that hasn't got at least one member working behind the barbed wire . . . That keeps people quiet . . .'

On top of this the region is feeling the full force of the crisis currently besetting other sectors of the economy. Major local concerns are going under. The Amiot naval shipyard is threatened with closure. The dairy industry is regrouping, and the CIT-Alcatel company, which manufactures telephone-exchange equipment, has announced the closure of several of its factories. That means that the only jobs available locally are with COGEMA or with the companies servicing the nuclear site. It is the sort of situation that can stifle a lot of anger and silence many fears. The militant members of the anti-nuclear protest movement know all about this. Their ranks are thin nowadays, and many a former environmentalist is trying to draw a veil over his past in order that he or his son can get a job at the plant.

> The problem is the crisis and people's fear of unemployment. How many who once led protest marches are today working for COGEMA! But now the anti-nuclear campaigners daren't even demonstrate any more, because even they don't know whether they might not need to work there themselves one day!

Beyond these paternalistic visions of the world of the reprocessing plant, Hagar society remains riddled with cracks through which discontent, bitterness, and resentment are always welling up: 'The plant has ruined this as a place to live. Now folk who work at the plant are at odds with us farmers. When you walk into a café in your muddy boots and your work clothes . . . They'll stare at you . . . You'll be lucky to get served!' And again: 'It's the atmosphere between people that's changed. Folk don't get together any more . . .'

This state of rupture between groups with divergent occupational interests and concerns is reinforced by the fact that SGN and COGEMA are currently developing a veritable company culture that effectively isolates their employees from the rest of the population.

Both the *Grand chantier* and the plant offer their workers on site all the services they require to organise their day-to-day existence. Banks, post offices, insurance agencies, and social-security offices are all laid on for them so that they never need to use the often overloaded local services in the places where they live. Through the medium of a joint works council, employees of the various companies involved in the *Grand chantier* and their families have access to some fifteen sports, a lending library, and various clubs of a cultural nature. People who work for COGEMA enjoy similar opportunities, likewise through their works council, plus various social advantages for themselves and their families including holiday camps for the children, language courses abroad, family tours, and even special loans.

The la Hague plant and its extension in the *Grand chantier* form an autonomous, self-contained entity, a kind of 'super municipality' within the canton. It is the most populous, and it is also the wealthiest (which endows it with a mysterious power). Above all, its employees enjoy such conspicuous advantages (not to mention higher pay coupled with allowances for, among other things, marriage, child-birth, moving house, and non-residence) that traditional solidarities in this deeply egalitarian region have simply collapsed.

Moreover, when the management of the plant decides to hold an 'Open Day', it invites only its own employees and their families. Everyone else, be they farmers, craft-tradesmen, municipal officers, or local shopkeepers, it keeps away as if they were the new have-nots in this society of haves. An apparently innocuous policy is in fact having the effect of widening one of the gulfs that today divide the population of la Hague.

Split between those who still earn their living by the old trades and those involved in this new world of high technology, torn apart by wage differentials that undermine traditional solidarities, fragmented into clans that hold conflicting ideological convictions, into communities of immigrants belonging to different nationalities and speaking different languages, and into groups of French men and women from all over the country and Normans from other parts of the province, Hagar society has, as it were, become exploded into a series of independent, mutually exclusive nuclei.

Weather and rumour

These contiguous yet apparently in every way distinct societies nevertheless share a common preoccupation: trying to live next door to this place where substances are handled that are or have been used to manufacture bombs (because that is still very much the public perception of the nuclear industry).

Asked 'What does nuclear energy mean to you?', ten-year-olds in a Beaumont primary-school class chorused: 'War, the bomb . . .' Only subsequently were other matters mentioned, other justifications for the use of *le nucléaire*.

In the minds of these children who have never known war, as in the minds of many adults who say they no longer believe in a nuclear war, the atom is still bracketed with the bomb. The words 'nuclear' and 'atomic' are forever synonymous with violent explosions, terrifying destruction, appalling consequences. It is as if the first explosion at Hiroshima, which for the uninformed public marked the emergence of the new energy, remained inextricably bound up with it. The civil nuclear industry is still paying the price for its military parentage.

It is also true that cinema has seized on the nuclear apocalypse,[7] detailing in feature films and documentaries the death-dealing effects proceeding from that first splitting of the atom, revealing or imagining the implications that flow from it as regards the destiny of mankind and of our world. The cinema polishes myth, provides discourse, and feeds the imaginations of societies.

To neglect this link that has been forged for ever between nuclear energy and war, together with the charge of fantasy that it generates, is to invite rebuff and encourage potentially irreparable misunderstandings between those whose decision it is to harness this form of energy and those on whom it is imposed. We saw in France quite recently how the accident at the Chernobyl power station resulted in a reversal of national opinion, which had traditionally been in favour of the civil nuclear industry.[8]

In our Western societies the lethal birth and the novelty of nuclear energy have meant that this whole area is subject to constant probing by the media. It is the focus of interminable arguments and debates in which each protagonist sticks rigidly to his or her position. As a result, for those who do not know what to believe or which side to line up on, the nuclear phenomenon will forever bear the mark of ambivalence and ambiguity.

At la Hague there is no escaping the ambiguous atmosphere that surrounds nuclear energy. However, no one talks about it. These features of the history of the nuclear industry are never referred to in order, for example, to express a fear of living in the vicinity of such establishments. Chernobyl did not trigger any anxiety syndrome or panic reaction among the local population. Yet people here were aware, contrary to what was being said in Paris, that 'the cloud from Chernobyl passed right over la Hague ... My father works at COGEMA, and suddenly the sirens went off, sounding the alarm: it was the Chernobyl cloud going over ...'

Nevertheless, people will state emphatically: 'Chernobyl couldn't happen here,' adding for their own reassurance: 'Better precautions are taken in France, fortunately ... because they are dangerous, these plants ...'

Opinion polls show that fear of an accident like that at Chernobyl appears less acute, the nearer a person lives to a nuclear establishment.[9] At la Hague, people act as they do elsewhere, denying that they ever drew a parallel between the accident at the Soviet power station and the la Hague plant. I put the question: 'After Chernobyl, didn't it occur to you that ...?' The answer came back: 'No, you see we've got our roots here, we don't think too much ... it's funny ...' This lethargy of memory is coupled with an element of fatalism: 'You can't think about it all the time, you wouldn't be living ... If we were in constant fear of that, we'd soon be packing our bags!'

The same phenomena (turning a blind eye and denying the risk) that we find among workers at the plant also occur among those who live nearby: 'Everything's taken care of here ... There's no danger, or it would need a plane to crash on the plant ...'

However, these denials do not suffice to give complete reassurance to the populations that live in the vicinity of such sites. To protect themselves against them, people will exploit every means and cite every argument that presents itself, be it the topography of their territory, or the economic advantages that flow from the installation and continued operation of these establishments, or even fate, which requires man to put up with a reality against which he is powerless to do anything: 'What do you expect us to do now? The plant's there, we have to live with it.'

But there is something more, it seems to me, than this litany of arguments. Among local people one occasionally becomes aware of a buried anxiety, a latent fear – misgivings, in a word, which borrow the moaning of the wind or the mouth of rumour to voice themselves.

Native or *horsain*, everyone at la Hague nowadays complains about the weather: 'If I leave here, it won't be on account of "that", it'll be on account of the weather,' said a farmer's wife whose family had always lived at la Hague, while the mayor of one village confirmed: 'If people leave here it's not because they're afraid but because of the weather.'

It is as if, for the people of la Hague, the climate that is so characteristic of their region (mild, with no great temperature differentials, but changeable, with wind and rain giving way to wonderful sunny spells in which waves of irridescent light break over the sea and the countryside) had suddenly become more than they can bear, to the point where they attribute all their ills to it. We are talking about things that their ancestors endured for generations: the persistent fog that hangs over Beaumont, snagging on and weeping from the dripstones of the roofs, the leaden skies that suddenly part to let the sun shine gloriously through, the easterly wind that whitens the crests of the waves out in the tide race, enabling people to forecast tomorrow's weather, the rain that is so familiar that their dialect distinguishes at least thirteen different types of it,[10] and a host of other meteorological features that poets have seized on to celebrate the uniqueness of their *pays*:

Song of the wind, thinly, subtly
Smelling so good, smelling of newness,
When spring is green on the hillsides
And the flowers still tiny.

Song of the wind, winter's song,
Of the wind that moans, the wind that whistles,
That stirs mankind, whips up the sea,
Makes foam spit and splatter.

Song of the wind, song of forever,
Coming and going, living and dying,
Rising again with each new dawn.
How I love to watch the clouds scud across the sky.[11]

Today, however, all these climatic features, all this atmospheric raw material out of which the Hagar identity has been fashioned over the centuries, are subjects of perpetual complaint, seized on as pretexts for leaving the ancestral homeland.

In this context of modernity, this high-tech atmosphere ushered in by the plant, people's links with the environment are loosening. The close ties that Hagars used to have with nature are breaking down. The weather, the wind, the rain and fog, the low cloud, squalls, storms, and all the other natural phenomena about which folk complain do indeed reveal that a civilisation, their civilisation, is dying.

Is it the contagion of the newcomers who, while acknowledging the remarkable beauty of the area, regret having to put up with its windy, rainy climate, which sees so little sun and knows so few really warm days? Or is it the influence of the women who live such isolated lives in the new villages or have too little privacy in the modular developments and who, drifting between boredom and depression, point the finger at 'the weather' as being to blame for the feelings of uneasiness that are virtually endemic among them? 'In some villages the women who arrived recently are bored, and then they sap the morale of the other women, the local women, who would never have noticed that they were bored but for them!'

There is no doubt that the two camps (old inhabitants and new residents) influence each other. However, if everyone complains so bitterly about the 'dreadful weather', it is because the weather provides them with a common language, a convenient code (which has the added advantage of being quite a fashionable lingo in an age where the talk is all of leisure activities and holidays in the sun) for saying, without actually using the words: 'I've got to get away from this awful place!'

The rumours that do the rounds at la Hague retail the same admission: this place is dangerous.

Rumours circulate incessantly on the plateau. Tales imported from elsewhere, from other regions and other countries, blend with the stories that locals whisper among themselves. All of them, however, convey the same dread of *le nucléaire*.

The distant rumours that Hagars pick up from visiting journalists or passing holidaymakers tell them the sorts of thing the outside world says about la Hague, how 'children are born deformed there . . . Calves have two heads . . . The cows' milk is contaminated and is thrown away every day after milking . . .'

The farther afield the rumourmongers hail from, the more improbable or fantastic the rumours become. They seem to swell in proportion to the distance between their point of origin and the epicentre where the events they purport to deal with took place.

Hagars make fun of the more fantastic claims. Nevertheless, the mere fact that such stories are able to spread confirms them in the notion that they live in the vicinity of what is by no means a neutral location. It is the same with rumours that are known to be false as with the rest: something always sticks.

As for their own rumours, the ones that the people of la Hague whisper among themselves, they suggest that strange things go on 'up there' and that, some day or other, living there will cost them their lives.

Every incident or mishap occurring anywhere near the site is promptly attributed to *le nucléaire*.

One morning in April 1988 the eels in the stream that descends from the plateau were found dead. A rumour promptly took wing: 'It's due to nuclear contamination.' Publication of the analyses carried out by various commissions was to show that this was not so at all. It was a case of chemical pollution caused by soda having been poured into the stream, probably by one of the firms employed on the *Grand chantier*.

One night in October 1987, following heavy rain, the sleepy river that winds along the bottom of the valley of les Cannivières, which cuts through the plateau, suddenly swelled and turned into a torrent of mud. It laid waste everything in its path, bursting into the houses along its banks and forcing the inhabitants to take refuge upstairs. One old lady was drowned. An explanation of the origin of that mass of water that came rushing down from the plateau and swept into the valley is still being sought. But rumour lost no time in insinuating: 'The plant was to blame. It was all the water they had dammed up there suddenly bursting through the walls . . .'

This direct accusation subsequently attracted what for some constituted a more explicit explanation of the great flood. 'There are rats up there . . . It's common knowledge . . . So they decided to have a purge

... Then afterwards they had to get rid of the rats, and that was how they flushed them away.'

In other words, the water that came rushing down from the plateau was the result of cleaning out that enormous dustbin. Hercules cleaned out the Augean stables; *le nucléaire* was cleaning out its own.

It is true that rats have invaded the plant and have been followed by all kinds of pests and predators. This is confirmed by members of the plant's health and safety committee:

> Rats do get into the buildings, but we deal with the problem in the usual way, by putting down rat poison. There are cats, too, which are contaminated and which pass on contamination ... They're hunted as well, but we've found other people feeding them ... There've been rabbits, too ... I've seen people hunting rabbits in the plant. I don't know if they ate them afterwards ... We found mice in the women's toilets recently ...

From there a whole world of rumour began to fuse, playing in every register simultaneously: truth and imagination, topography, the vastness of the site, the disgust inspired by rodents, the suggestive powers of certain nouns, and deep, repressed fears. Gradually this disturbing vessel moored up on the plateau came to be colonised by a no less disturbing fauna! Ought these rumours of mopping up foul beasts to be seen as a way of taming the nuclear phenomenon or as the expression of a hidden anxiety?

The rumours come and go. Some will flare up in the wake of an incident, then die down again, stifled by official denials and press releases. Others are more persistent: having once materialised, they never die. Passed on by long-time residents to the newcomers, handed down from the old to the young, they run and run. An example is the rumour alluding to the way la Hague would be evacuated in the event of a major accident.

An ORSEC-RAD plan was drawn up at the time the plant was commissioned. However, the plan, which covers the whole *département*, has never been published. Responsibility for activating it and carrying it through rests with the prefect, aided by a special staff. Although no one knows officially what the plan contains, rumour has it that:

> It's complete nonsense. The reason why they don't want to show it to anyone is that they're afraid people will misunderstand it and will panic. In the plan the only people requisitioned are the police and the army ... What do you think that's for? To stop people leaving, that's what ... Getting out of here ...

In addition, copies of a little green book entitled PPI (*Plan particulier d'intervention* or 'special plan of operation') were sent to all the town halls of the canton, which distributed it to the inhabitants. The green book lists the instructions to be followed in case of accident. If confinement is ordered, 'go home, hermetically seal doors, windows, and other ventilation systems', then 'stay watching television or listening to the radio'. If a decision is taken to evacuate, the populations affected should 'gather in families and pack their toilet things and a change of clothes and footwear in a large plastic bag or dustbin liner, well sealed. Coaches will pick those populations up, and they will be evacuated and subsequently regrouped for the purposes of control and registration . . .'

On the basis of these laconic instructions, rumours started to materialise:

> If there's a minor accident you have to stay at home and wait for someone to come and get you . . . If there's a major accident you have to assemble on the main road and wait to be picked up . . .

> There's one plan for evacuating the livestock and another for the people . . . It's a con, it'll never work . . .

> I'll tell you one thing, they'll never evacuate us . . . One fine day they'll cut off the headland [*on coupera la pointe*] . . . They'll just leave us here!

> Folk down at Carentan will flood the marshes again to stop the radiation victims getting through. It's easy, you blow up two or three dykes, nothing to it . . .

> We know perfectly well we've had it here. If anything happens, they'll dump us. The lepers of the Cotentin, that's what we are!

From memories of the last war to the nuclear apocalypse is but a step, and it is one that rumour takes lightly. Same causes, same effects, runs the popular wisdom.

Beyond the facts of history, fiction springs. Statements about la Hague being 'set adrift' and the idea that 'they'll cut the bridges with the mainland' appeal to the imagination of the Hagars, whose gaze has always been turned towards the sea and distant horizons as if they were immemorially imbued with regret at being only an 'almost-island' (as the French call a peninsula; Tr.). That is what they mean when they say: 'We're pretty cut off here, but we're open on three sides . . .'

The nuclear apocalypse brings them confirmation of their destiny, which according to them is to become islanders. Even in terms of rumour, people hear only what they expect to hear.

Amazingly, we have to go right back to the primary myth, the foundation myth, to understand why these men and women so easily allowed a nuclear reprocessing plant to be installed on their moorland!

Rumour is a form of social communication, enabling members of different groups to talk to one another and give common voice to their dread of unanswered questions. It is only in and through rumour that this shattered society speaks in unison.

Lastly (and this is by no means the least of its advantages) rumour exasperates 'them', the ones who claim to be in possession of the truth. 'Do people here still believe that the marshes will be flooded to stop them getting out if there's an accident?' I was asked by an astonished senior executive at the plant. What could I say? He need only have listened to the rumours.

3   The politics of nuclear power

There would be one way to cut short the rumours, and it would be for the management of the plant to speak plainly about the industrial policy it intends to pursue as well as about pollution or about safety problems with partners whom it regarded and who regarded themselves as equals. But with whom should it hold such a dialogue? With the local populations? Twenty years of mutual distrust are not easily forgotten. With local politicians? A history of passivity and submissiveness is not easily overcome. With the groups that opposed and still oppose the spread of the nuclear industry? But would they be able to drop their futile demonstrations, their abortive campaigns, their whole discredited struggle? And what of the technocrats? Do they think they will simply be able to disregard their aversion to all who oppose them? The public, the politicians, the anti-nuclear lobby, each one of these groups might have constituted a countervailing power to the real or imagined hold that COGEMA has on the region. None of them wanted to or has managed to. In the circumstances, is there any hope at all, here at la Hague, of finding a forum of discussion and communication, a space for mutual recognition?[1]

Communication at cross-purposes

'The whole problem stems from the fact that people here were taken in, so they no longer believe what they're told. I'm from la Hague myself . . . and when la Hague folk have been duped, it's a long, hard struggle to win back their confidence.'

The story of communications between the industrial authorities and the local population is one long chapter of missed opportunities.

So far as the public is concerned, distrust of COGEMA is the rule as regards information.

In the beginning, when the Parisian authorities came to present the original industrial-development project, there was mention only of a plant to manufacture plutonium. Local residents subsequently became aware that this involved reprocessing waste and that they had in effect given permission for the installation, up there on the moor, of a *dustbin* in which the world's nuclear detritus was now piling up.

Since making this discovery, which may appear ridiculous in the technocrat's eyes but not to the mayors of the canton nor to those who recall the highly undemocratic circumstances in which the plant was foisted on them, the people of la Hague feel that they have been had. The feeling became even stronger after COGEMA had taken charge, because the company proved quite incapable, at least in the early days, of establishing confidential relations with the public or managing the incidents that occurred on the site in any coherent fashion. Let me cite as proof of this the accounts of certain occurrences that might have had disastrous consequences for the local inhabitants. Though they happened some years back, our interviewees constantly came out with them in identically vehement tones tinged with barely suppressed anger. They have almost achieved the status of symbolic events. Invariably dated with precision, they will forever punctuate the collective memory of the group like so many marks of the duplicity of the industrial authorities.

In January 1980 the five-kilometre long outflow pipe into the sea was found to be broken a hundred metres from the shore.

> The pipe carries the waste-bearing water out into the Blanchard Race, which has a very powerful current . . . There were some storms . . . The pipe, which is supposed to discharge far out in the race, had become corroded and was discharging a hundred metres from the shore . . . The manager said at that time: 'It's hardly surprising because this winter we've had storms of more than sixty kilometres an hour [gale force]!' But everyone hereabouts knows you get storms of a hundred and thirty, a hundred and forty [hurricane force]! So why wasn't that allowed for? I tell you, I know people who haven't collected shellfish or been shrimping that way since. They don't dare to now!

On 15 April 1980 fire broke out in two mains transformers. The central circuit and the auxiliary circuit alongside it were both damaged, and the plant was left without electricity. Ventilation in the workshops stopped, and the cooling circuits in the tanks containing the high-level waste cut out. Generators from the Arsenal had to be sent for urgently. 'We were within an ace of a major accident,' the plant manager admitted later. Yet no preventative measures had been taken to ensure the safety of surrounding populations who might have had to be evacuated. 'We knew nothing about it! It was afterwards we found out, they never tell us anything, we don't know anything!'

On 6 January 1981 fire broke out in an outlying storage silo. The fire smouldered for hours, releasing a radioactive cloud that contaminated vehicles standing in a car park. The alarms at the exit gate were set off as the cloud of radioactive fumes went past, yet contaminated cars and employees were allowed out. This accident, like the earlier one, became known only as a result of revelations by militant trade unionists at the plant.

> And above all there's the secrecy! Take the silo fire. Nothing was said, and that was a real disaster, that was. The wind was from the north-west, blowing towards Herqueville, Beaumont practically . . . But above all on the plant, on the car park where the vehicles became contaminated. That must have been on a Friday. The next day I was leaving for Grenoble on business. I went off, came back a week later, and that was when I found out my car had been contaminated. I'd been trailing it all around everywhere . . . It's monstrous! And when you think there was this bloke who let everybody through without saying anything, and there was no disciplinary action, nothing . . . Maybe he even got a pat on the back. They certainly knew about it up there, the alarms went off. But that means confining everybody, and there'd be panic . . . Women seeing their husbands not come home . . . So they let people go.
>
> But there'll be a worse panic now because then they let people go when it wasn't too bad, the contamination. Now if they're confined people are going to panic and say: 'This is really serious, this is a catastrophe, if they're confining people like that!' And people may start wondering up to what point they're going to allow them to become contaminated.
>
> Basically, that's what's so serious – the secrecy. Rather than giving people confidence by saying every time there's an alert: 'Everything's being taken care of.' Nowadays people are afraid of not being told a thing, of incidents being played down!

The silo fire, which people talk about constantly at la Hague, undermined COGEMA's credibility for a long time.[2] Even today sour jokes are told about the statement made after the fire by the then manager of the plant that 'no significant contamination carried farther than the perimeter of the establishment'!

Popular irony, throwing up a pathetic rampart against an inexpressible fear, has turned the statement around and announces that 'the fence stops the nuclear, the manager said so'!

Since then, local residents have been convinced that what happens at the plant is kept from them, or at least that they will learn of it only in roundabout ways. They feel that, whatever they do, they are excluded from and have no control over the sources of information and knowledge. Such beliefs, one feels, reinforce the rumours circulating to the effect that 'they'll never evacuate us' and that Hagars are 'the lepers of the Cotentin'.

Despite the enhanced safety measures adopted in the wake of these accidents, locals live in fear that they are being kept in ignorance of what could happen at the plant. They suspect that their environment is gradually being allowed to become contaminated without their knowing anything about it. 'That's the biggest worry! You can say to yourself at any given moment, if something goes wrong we won't be told ... That's the greatest fear that people living around here can have ... How much, if anything does go wrong one day, will they be told?'

The laconic, technically worded bulletin that, since the silo fire, the management of the plant has published in the local press each week is too lofty in tone to do anything to alter this view. 'No one reads the bulletin! They never say anything in it, or if they do it's played down!'

The secrecy surrounding the measurements that are taken almost daily at various points throughout la Hague, relating to everyday foodstuffs as well as to air and water, confirms local residents in their impression of being passed over so far as information is concerned. 'They monitor everything, the milk, the fish ... but we don't see the findings. They don't tell us anything and you mustn't ever say anything or ask questions.'

Once a year the mayors of the canton receive the results of the monitoring operation carried out by the Paris-based SCPRI (*Service centrale de protection contre les rayonnements ionisants*) on fallout on the sea, on the land, and in the water. Highly technical and not at all suitable for a wide audience, these dossiers are for the most part carefully filed away in local-government record offices. The scientists having made no attempt to find a comprehensible language and an accessible style of presentation for such data, the mayors prefer not to make them public in order to get out of having to answer questions or to avoid reminding their constituents that they live in a monitored area.

Communication is more than an abstract arrangement for producing statements that claim to represent knowledge and truth and require to be accepted as such. It also involves identifying the levels of reception and modes of acceptance of those utterances in the culture for which they are intended. In the absence of such an operation, the process of exchange, the relationship implicit in communication, cannot come about. The arrogance of the one party and the subordination of the other give rise to misunderstanding, and the cycle of secrecy engages from both sides.

The recent revelations taken up by the national and local press regarding the true severity of the Three Mile Island accident and the one that occurred at Windscale in north-west England back in 1957, followed by the US Department of Energy's cynical admission that it had deliberately allowed the nuclear installation at Fernald, Ohio, to leak for more than twenty years, were not calculated to change people's minds.[3] Of course, none of these 'affairs' is talked about outside anti-nuclear circles (any more than the Chernobyl accident), as if silence made it possible to forget and bury fear.

In this context of secrecy and of information that is assumed to be biased, the most insignificant event can strengthen people's feeling of being dominated and manipulated by higher powers. In the late 1970s new sirens appeared on local town-hall roofs. Not even the mayors were able to say who had given orders for them to be placed there or who was to activate them. But people immediately started muttering that if sirens were being put up it meant that an accident was expected and that undoubtedly 'things are going badly up there'. Eventually, it emerged that the order in question dated from before the last war; an administration that was nothing if not persistent had at last got around to implementing it. 'People don't think any more, they're just scared, that's all there is to it.'

An everyday, habitual fear haunts la Hague. It hides behind defence mechanisms of all kinds, ranging from assertions of blind confidence in the industrial authorities, via indifference, passivity, and a general flight from knowledge, all the way to a permanent scepticism with regard to all information emanating from 'up there'. Be they submissive or rebellious, grave or apparently insouciant, the inhabitants of this place are all prey to the same anguish, the same underlying uncertainty.

From the point of view of the industrial authorities, this is a disappointment. Particularly over the last few years they have been trying to reduce the gap that still exists between what they say and the way in which it is received by the population or its elected representatives. 'How,' the plant manager wonders, 'do we get the message across to the public about how harmless the nuclear industry is? I have the elected representatives, the district councillors, in once a year. We take stock, I show them the latest installations. But there aren't many questions. They have a strong sense of status and rank, you see, and we're scientists!'

The gap that remains and that distresses the industrial authorities is perhaps due less to the fact that the people of la Hague have a strong sense of rank than to the fact that the message they are being offered leaves little room for discussion, simply affirming a priori what they are asking to have proved, namely that the nuclear industry is *harmless*. It is precisely that harmlessness that, consciously or unconsciously, everyone questions. If communication does not take place it is because both sides stick rigidly to their positions, unable or unwilling to understand each other.

Communication is able to create social bonds only to the extent to which it is governed by a logic of equivalence.

Politicians under pressure

The avenues of dialogue might have passed through the *district*, a political organism representing the nineteen municipalities of the canton and therefore capable in practice of discussing matters with COGEMA representatives.

In January 1976 the la Hague plant became a corporate entity subject to private law and as such liable to pay personnel tax to the municipality. This consequence did not pass unnoticed by the prefectural administration, which lost no time in pointing out to the canton's mayors that it would be in their interest to set up a federative body capable of levying and allocating the taxes paid by the various *Grand chantier* companies and by COGEMA, taxes that would otherwise flow exclusively into the coffers of the municipalities in which the plant was actually situated. The institution advocated was a district, which offered the advantage of making it possible to group services together while still respecting the autonomy of the municipalities.

> In 1976, between Christmas and New Year, the Sub-Prefect did the rounds of all the town halls telling people 'You must form a district. Then you'll have first claim on the revenue from the personnel tax paid by the plant.' We'd be first in line for such taxes. Asked how much the tax amounted to, he said: 600 million. So I said; 'We can't say no.' You don't turn down a windfall like that – my citizens would have torn me to pieces!

The district of la Hague canton was officially registered in February 1977.

It is administered by a council made up of delegates from the individual municipal councils and by an executive consisting of a chairman and three vice-chairmen elected in council. The district enjoys financial autonomy; that is to say, it is authorised to levy taxation in the same way as the municipality in a proportion determined by the general council of the *département*. The district council appoints sub-committees from within its ranks to look into matters submitted to the council and to furnish it with all necessary advice and observations. There are three of these sub-committees (finance, public works, and general administration), and through them the district is competent to deliberate in a number of areas of regional life: town and country planning, highways, socio-educational, cultural, and sports facilities, cleaning, drinking-water supply, fire brigades, and so on.

These operating methods and these wide-ranging powers might have enabled the district to play an organising or at least a unifying role in the life of the canton and to mediate between the local population and the management of the plant. Not a bit of it.

Since the district was set up in 1977, three councils have been elected, following the pattern of local-government elections with the resultant changes of political coloration. You will hear it said, for example, that, right from the second council, 'opponents of the nuclear industry were in the majority and decided about the elected officers'. While it is true that the most recent councils have taken up rather different positions with regard to the developments requested by the municipalities to meet the influx of population, the fact remains that they have always stated their determination not to constitute an authority responsible for considering and co-ordinating the future of the canton.

> The district isn't some kind of super-municipality! We must above all guard against that, and its chairman is not a super-mayor. The district was created in order to tap tax revenue that would otherwise have benefited only four municipalities. However, the municipalities are still free to decide what they want. The district has the finance and the municipalities request that such-and-such a project be financed. Basically, we're the provider of funds and principal contractor . . .

That is how the current chairman sums up the general direction of district policy.

When work began on extending the plant in 1980, which meant setting up a great many off-site facilities, the *Grand chantier* co-ordinator did not approach the cantonal assembly for a decision about where to put them but dealt directly with the municipalities. No overall debate about rational development of the region took place at district level. The district council had only to take cognisance of and process the various infrastructure requests submitted by the municipalities, confining itself to monitoring the sizes of the loans allocated, correcting appeals procedures with regard to tenders, and then seeing that the work was properly carried out. In other words, the district was kept (and above all kept itself) entirely apart from the massive enterprise represented by the *Grand chantier*.

The first district council authorised the construction of many municipal facilities, the appropriateness of which was closely bound up with the exigencies imposed by the plant extension, without concerning itself overmuch with what would happen to them and who would run them once the *Grand chantier* was completed. The second district council, elected in 1983, called a halt to this wholesale amenity programme and concentrated on managing what had been built and attempting to assess the long-term burden on the budgets of local communities. To help this management project to fruition, the council made its policy more municipality oriented by adopting two specific measures.

The first was designed to change the number of delegates from the municipalities who sat on the council. The 1977 bye-laws had provided for each municipality to be represented on the council by one delegate, with additional delegates being added as a function of the size of the municipal population. Municipalities with over 800 inhabitants had three additional delegates, municipalities with over 400 inhabitants had two, and municipalities with over 200 inhabitants had one. In July 1983 the district council voted to change this pattern of representation. In future each municipality would be represented by three delegates, with one additional delegate for municipalities of between 801 and 1,200 inhabitants, two for municipalities of between 1,201 and 1,600 inhabitants, and three for municipalities with between 1,601 and 3,200 inhabitants. The official explanation provided by the sub-committee responsible for procedures cited the impossibility of delegates from small municipalities participating in the work of all the committees, as the rules required. This meant that they had to resort to substitutes or more municipal councillors in order to keep pace with all the committee business. These took no part in council debates, of course. Clearly, however, the effect of increased municipal representation on the council was to reduce the importance of the larger municipalities, which might have been tempted to exercise a certain hegemony by creating their own clientele. In other words, the change can be seen as an attempt to neutralise the larger municipalities more effectively. Added to which, the two most populous municipalities in the canton, which had hitherto commanded the largest number of delegates, were both headed by mayors who worked for COGEMA!

The second decision, taken at the very beginning of the council's second term, was of a formal nature. It consisted in offering each municipality an annual budget, determined on the basis of its current requirements, the work it plans to carry out, the expenses it has to manage, and its population. In return the municipality must respect these budgetary constraints while remaining free to make whatever choices it sees fit within them. The district does not interfere with judgements as to the appropriateness of those choices. The purpose of this arrangement is to increase the power of the municipality not only *vis-à-vis* other municipalities but also *vis-à-vis* the district council, which might have been tempted to interfere in municipal affairs. The secretary-general of the district explains, for example, that delegates:

> are elected by their municipal council to look after the interests of their municipality at district level. In those sectors where the district interferes, it does so at the behest of the municipality. There is no transfer of powers from municipality to district, and in fact what we have noticed is that, whatever you do, without the backing of the local elected representatives it won't work. Reorganising a school, building only one village hall for adjacent municipalities ... If the elected representatives don't like it, nothing can be imposed. The municipalities retain full autonomy, and it's up to the elected representative.

He adds:

There are nineteen municipalities there side by side, voicing the occasional opinion about their next-door neighbour ... But be careful, they tell themselves, because afterwards you're going to be putting forward your own plan ... so ... watch what you say!

The only services that the district runs at cantonal level are water, domestic-refuse collection, and the fire brigade. In all other sectors the municipality retains full autonomy. Apart from these public services and one or two other matters that concern the canton (school buses, grants to various associations or committees operating at cantonal level), the district has never put on its agenda a discussion about the problems faced by the canton as a whole in connection with the la Hague plant and its ramifications. Neither planning on the peninsula, nor transport, nor co-ordinated school-building, much less the problem of public safety for those living in the vicinity of these high-risk establishments, has hitherto been discussed, and it is difficult to see how they might be discussed in future. In the context of the kind of policy currently championed at district level, it is clear that any councillor, no matter what his political persuasion, who tried to place such matters on the agenda would be turned down straight by his colleagues.

For there to be any political discussion at district level, the district council would have to be elected by universal suffrage, which is not the case. There's no stable majority on the district council. You might have a group of municipalities get together to see a particular piece of business through, but next time that'll be it!

Trying to get one of these general questions placed on the agenda, questions that concern all the municipalities involved, or trying to encourage discussion about the safety of the canton's populations is tantamount, in the vocabulary of the local elected representatives, to 'indulging in politics', which is something they say they are determined not to do. 'Above all we can't have politics coming into district affairs,' I was told repeatedly. This position is so entrenched that at the time of the last general election the majority of the council refused to allow the district hall to be used for election meetings. 'It's a local-government building and not to be used for public meetings, especially not political ones!'

At district level the general assumption is that discussion of these matters of public interest would inevitably lead to confrontations between pro- and anti-nuclear elements, between those councillors who opposed the extension of the plant and those who supported it. In the eyes of most councillors, such discussions are tarnished with 'politics' (in the sense of 'prejudice'), but above all many of them are afraid of irritating COGEMA, dispenser of the fattest loans and inescapable partner so far as managing the district's debt burden is concerned. 'There's no debate at district because there are those who think that wanting to call COGEMA to account on safety or anything else is a bit like biting the hand that feeds you.'

The elected representatives of la Hague want none of this kind of confrontation, public speechifying, and aggressive requesting of information. Yet there is no doubt that, had they got together and presented a common front, they would have succeeded in setting up a countervailing power to that automatically and somewhat mysteriously exerted by COGEMA purely by virtue of its dominance over the regional economy.

To voice their mistrust and give expression to their fears about the future, local politicians chose a strategy of falling back under cover of darkness, as it were. It was by making secret, almost clandestine preparations for the elections of the officers of the second district council that the so-called 'anti-nuclears' managed to get the candidates of their choice elected, keeping out the mayors of the largest municipalities and those too conspicuously loyal to COGEMA: 'Before the elections of the officers we all convened, all the la Hague councillors who thought the same way and got on well together ... We met one night at a large, secluded farm to agree prior to the district-council meeting. We decided what had to be done, and it went off just the way we'd said!'

The members of the second district council were then able to decide about the granting of the budget, which leaves the municipalities with their autonomy intact but constitutes a policy of, in effect, hiding one's head in the sand. Granted, the municipality may decide to resist the advances of the modern world, or it may on the contrary choose to welcome that world with open arms. But as long as this policy is in place no project on a cantonal scale nor any kind of joint initiative can be envisaged. Dug in behind its official boundaries, confined to its own territory, the municipality remains in sole charge of its destiny. But has it the power to assume that charge?

On this isolated promontory in the grip of the technological revolution, the local elected representatives are not making the best use of their power and of the institutional resources available to them to foster a regional policy and establish the kind of countervailing force that would have made it obligatory for the industrial invaders to talk to them.

On this fog-bound extremity of Europe, a continent that is concerned only with abolishing frontiers, encouraging the free circulation of ideas, and promoting dialogue among men, we find a paradoxical reaffirmation of a kind of local-government autonomy that one thought was gone for ever. La Hague has reinvented the municipality, the *commune*, as if this unit were capable, unaided, of throwing up a rampart against the invasion of the modern world and the attendant loss of identity.

The anti-nuclear campaign

The campaign against the nuclear industry's invasion and conquest of the region did not always have the muffled, hidden character that it presents today. There was a time when everything to do with nuclear energy, whether it was the construction of Flamanville power station or the extension of the la Hague plant, triggered conflict and aroused mass opposition.

Granted, the people of la Hague have never exactly constituted the spearhead of the anti-nuclear campaign, but certain local politicians and one or two members of old and influential families have played an active part in it. The history of that campaign is worth recounting here in that it will help us to understand certain attitudes and modes of behaviour peculiar to the people of the peninsula.

Both within the canton and in the regions adjoining it, the early years of the nuclear era were quiet. We have seen how, with no direct consultation and no preliminary impact studies, the original plutonium-manufacturing plant was conceived and then imposed on the local population. No organised protest emerged at the time. Admittedly, opinions were divided from the outset. Some approved; others were disturbed. But no one went public with his fears or sought to foster any kind of grouping of opposition forces. The initiative for that came later, and it came from outside the canton.

The 1970s arrived. That was the period when protests were organised at nuclear power station sites all over France, the period that saw the emergence and organisation of environmental movements involving a rediscovery of nature coupled with a rejection of technology and its devastating legacy of pollution. In 1970 various groups came together in Cherbourg (left-of-centre politicians, teachers influenced by the events of May 1968, militant members of the environmental movements) to form a 'Committee Against Atomic Pollution in la Hague' (*Comité contre la pollution atomique dans la Hague*, CCPAH). The way the protagonists saw it, the committee was to function as an alarm network, carrying out a series of 'soft' actions or non-violent demonstrations and becoming a sort of pollution watchdog for the region. As early as 1974, however, there was talk of building a nuclear power station at Flamanville. From then on the actions of the committee focused on this part of the peninsula and above all became more radical, 'harder' in both word and deed. Not all sympathisers liked the change of direction, and this was when the prominent politicians who opposed any kind of violent action, finding themselves outnumbered by the more intransigent militants, resigned from the CCPAH. The committee, while still remaining independent, became affiliated to the 'Regional Anti-Nuclear Information and Campaigning Committee' (*Comité régional d'information et de luttes anti-nucléaires*, CRILAN), which operated throughout Lower Normandy and was itself simply a branch of the national committee.

Henceforth the anti-nuclear campaign in la Hague became part of the national struggle. It ceased to be a local matter, to be dealt with by local forces alone, and became a bone of contention like so many others in France. This broadening of the issue was not to everyone's liking and was undoubtedly responsible in part for the fact that the campaign has never really achieved a genuine popular base locally. At la Hague the social group tends to mobilise for concrete actions that have immediate local impact. The campaign against *le nucléaire* (an invisible form of pollution with remote, uncertain consequences), given that it was now also in the hands of 'outsiders', found little support among these rural communities.

One militant explains the failures encountered in the following terms:

> Farmers don't mobilise against the nuclear industry ... A plan to put a railway or a road across their land, though – that's a different story, then they'll do something. They've even come to us on occasion to ask for our help with that kind of campaign, because they regard us as professionals in the field of objecting. One of the mayors told us one day: 'We like you a lot, though we don't understand you.'

Another looks back reflectively at the shape of the campaign in the past:

> All through the struggle we've brandished the spectre of fear to get people mobilised. That may have damaged our case, particularly among farming folk who are very pragmatic and only believe in what they can see, apart from God ...

A struggle that is no longer purely local, a form of pollution that defies incorporation into familiar mental schemas, apocalyptic accounts that people are unable to situate in any logic of traditional time, these are all factors explaining why the local populations take so little part in the anti-nuclear fight. Mass support has come on only two occasions (at Flamanville, when the power station was being built, and at Cherbourg when the first ships arrived with imported spent fuel for reprocessing), only to slump as soon as the occasion had passed.

At Flamanville, everything seemed to favour the deployment of the anti-nuclear campaign. The power station had not yet been built, the mobilisation of certain population groups (notably the farmers) was effective, and the CCPAH believed it would win. A full programme of fêtes, exhibitions, protest marches, and public meetings was laid on in an attempt to make the people of Flamanville aware of the potential impact of the nuclear power station on the environment and on local life.

However, there was an economic crisis in the offing. In Flamanville, the men who had worked at the mine that had recently shut down were now unemployed, and the tradesmen saw their custom shrinking as people left the village. Both groups hoped that the building of the nuclear power station would provide fresh jobs and breathe new life into the place. In April 1975 a referendum was organised, and a majority said 'yes' to construction. Opponents of the power station refused to give in. They occupied the site night and day, and they set up an agricultural land organisation to try to spoil land deals. But it was no use. Anti-riot police laid siege to the site, and in 1976 the building began to rise on the amputated, disembowelled, shattered cliffs.

During 1975 the campaign against the construction of Flamanville power station had rather faded away, supplanted by events taking place on the la Hague site.

At the instigation of the CFDT (*Confédération française démocratique du travail*), then the majority trade union, workers at the la Hague plant reacted to the first rumours of privatisation in some original ways, including parading through the streets in 'shadock' suits (protective clothing worn by nuclear workers; see below, page 75), organising screenings in Beaumont, Cherbourg, and other places of the film *Doomed to Succeed*[4] (made by the CFDT shortly before this, the film, which gave a realistic account of working conditions in a nuclear environment, appeared most opportunely), and holding a conference on the nuclear industry staged in Cherbourg in November 1976, complete with an exhibition, lectures, and discussions.

As far as the workers were concerned, this was an exercise in popularisation. They wanted to make people aware of the special nature of their work and to explain that maintaining the highest possible safety standards at the plant was the only way of ensuring the safety of the neighbouring populations. It was their contention that such standards could not possibly be maintained in a private-enterprise operation geared to productivity and profit-making. Through these demonstrations, screenings, and exhibitions the uninformed public discovered to its amazement what *le nucléaire* was all about. They learned what it actually meant to work in a nuclear plant and handle radioactive substances. All the features peculiar to the nuclear industry (working 'on-limits', safety norms, the inconvenience of the special clothing required, the threat to the environment), which the scientists had been unable or unwilling to explain, the workers succeeded in bringing home to people in the space of a few days.

Was it a question of timing: were people perhaps better informed generally in late 1976 with regard to technological advances? Was it the visual pedagogy and techniques of dramatisation employed by the demonstrators? I could not say, but there is an abiding impression in everyone's memory of having 'grasped' what the nuclear phenomenon was all about at the time of those demonstrations, which was also the period of the great strike that broke out at the plant from September to December 1976. 'The most impressive times were '75–'76 ... the '76 strike ... When the fellows from la Hague brought the nuclear business off-site. They went marching through the streets in shadocks ... Then everyone became aware of what went on up there!'

Today there is no one left who does not know what goes on at the plant. It has ceased (in appearance, at least) to be a world apart, shrouded in secrecy. Nevertheless, as we have seen, neither the people who live nearby nor the men and women who work there will talk about it. Following that brief interlude of communication and mutual awareness, silence returned to cloak once more the dangerous tasks performed by vinyl-suited operators up on the plateau. It is just as if, to help them get through those tasks, it was felt necessary to surround the people who did them with a halo of calm. Unless of course folk are simply afraid that, if they make too much noise, if they stir up too much of a fuss, they may awaken dormant forces! You can never be too careful with *le nucléaire*.

The demonstrations and the strike, though well supported by the people of la Hague, were not enough to bring about a genuine popular uprising. That did not happen until the extension of the plant was mooted, involving at the same time the reprocessing of imported waste. Those plans did indeed lead large sections of the population, whether they lived near the plant or not, to demonstrate publicly against the nuclear industry's colonisation of the region. Militant groups, CFDT trade unionists, politicians of the Socialist and Communist parties, and purely anti-nuclear organisations (CRILAN, CCPAH) came together to form a 'Committee of Eighteen' to co-ordinate the campaign against the reprocessing of imported spent fuel.

In January 1979 the *Pacific Fisher* docked at Cherbourg bringing drums of nuclear waste from Japan. A mass public demonstration was organised to prevent the cargo from being unloaded. Between 6,000 and 7,000 people attended. Whole families went along, with women and children and even old men, moved by a wholly peaceful if somewhat xenophobic desire to prevent foreign waste from being disembarked on French soil. Police broke up the demonstration brutally. From then on only the militants, accompanied by a few determined anti-establishment youngsters, attempted to block the unloading of imported spent fuel. The campaign lost the popular, almost 'Sunday-afternoon' aspect it had once had, if only very briefly. In any case, according to the people we spoke to, public demonstrations are not something these Cotentin Normans make a habit of. Indeed, this very trait is often mentioned by way of furnishing a stereotypical alibi requiring no explanation and having the additional advantage of cutting off awkward questions: 'We don't make a big show of our opinions at la Hague, it's not done.'

This could be a smokescreen explanation enabling people to avoid owning up to a shameful element of xenophobia, because there is no getting away from the fact that genuine popular mobilisation occurred only when the demonstrations were directed against the unloading of spent fuel from other countries. In this part of Normandy, so readily hostile to *horsains*, the reprocessing of Japanese waste on home soil is regarded as intolerable. Yet the public is well aware that reprocessing (of French spent fuel) goes on at the plant in any case. So it may be that these allegedly xenophobic demonstrations are simply the outward indication of an unexpressed, unacknowledged fear.

After the harsh repression of the first popular demonstration, mass public actions became few and far between. The campaign moved into the political arena, with the baton being to some extent taken up by certain municipalities seeking by every available legal means to block the transport of waste through their territory.

> Listen to this: the mayor of Equeurdreville introduced a bye-law banning transit of the flasks unloaded at the docks. The prefect annulled it . . . So he introduced a bye-law banning lorries over five tons from driving through his municipality. The prefect annulled that one, too . . . The lorries went through eventually, but not before a great time had been had by all!

In Tonneville the mayor organised a vote on the question of reprocessing imported waste.

> In Tonneville we did a leaflet to explain that reprocessing had to go on, there was no choice, but that we didn't want to reprocess spent fuel from abroad. The question was 'Yes' to French reprocessing, 'No' to the reprocessing of foreign waste. We had a majority of 'Yes' votes. But it didn't change anything, did it? There's still imported waste up there!

Other municipalities organised referenda on their own initiative to try to block COGEMA's plans. In Omonville-la-Rogue and Saint-

Germain-des-Vaux the mayors asked their fellow-citizens to declare for or against the plant extension.

> In Omonville we put together a file and had a public exhibition. There was a police guard on it all! But people could find out what they wanted to know. I'd put together files on the water, on pollution, on agriculture ... I sent everything to the prefect afterwards. People voted. There was a majority against. But it was a very low turn-out. None of the people who work at the plant came and voted, they were afraid to, and even those who thought that one day their son or daughter might go to work at the plant didn't turn out either ... As for the stuff that went to the prefect, we never did find out what happened to it!

The fear of losing one's job by taking a stand in public and the spectre of large-scale unemployment are factors that influence all such consultation processes, topped by a feeling of impotence at fighting the bastions of the state.

> Never mind all the public-interest inquiries that were carried out, none of them did any good ... The conclusions were ignored. Their value was illusory. Take the inquiry about discharges ... Most municipalities demanded 'zero' discharges – gaseous discharges, that is. But they said: 'can't be done' ... and everyone accepted it. They're a submissive lot around here! And what about the high-tension line from Flamanville to la Hague? All the elected representatives were against it, all the municipal councils said 'no', so did the district and the regional council. For once everyone agreed that the thing should go underground or round by sea. But because they couldn't do it any other way, we got it all the same. But why, if technically they couldn't do it any other way, if that was the case, why ask us in the first place?'

This mistrust of the authorities that govern their territory, the fears inspired by the nature of the energy being handled inside those concrete buildings, and the worries that refuse to find expression in words all come out when the Hagar goes along to vote. In the cantonal elections held in March 1979, for the first time since 1955 the retiring councillor was re-elected only on the second ballot, with a mere 55.5 per cent of the votes cast compared with 45.5 per cent for the candidate who had campaigned under the slogan 'For the protection of la Hague' (*Pour la sauvegarde de la Hague*) and had the backing of the environmentalists. This initial warning acquired substance in March 1985 when the people of la Hague returned to the general council of the *département* the candidate who, though not nominated by the antinuclear movement and the environmentalists, had their support, beating the right-wing RPR (*Rassemblement pour la République*) candidate, who had been endorsed by the retiring councillor.

Meanwhile in 1980 the Nord-Cotentin constituency elected a Socialist MP who at that time opposed the projected extension of the plant. In 1981 the Socialists, having won the election, reneged on the promises they had made during the campaign. The government decided to honour the outgoing Prime Minister's signature on the order of 9 May 1981 authorising the plant extension. Contracts already entered into abroad were also at stake. In the ranks of the environmentalists and the anti-nuclear militants there was much disillusionment and a feeling that they had been had.

The alliance of trade union and environmentalist groups that had come about under the pressure of events now broke up. Their collaboration had in any case been neither understood nor accepted by many plant employees. The CFDT had the bitter experience of losing its majority in the next round of union elections. The various committees were disbanded, the militants dispersed, and the whole campaign ebbed. In a climate of virtually universal indifference, certain young militants sought to shake the local inhabitants out of their torpor by embarking on what were generally regarded as crazy escapades (blowing up a pylon, occupying a crane at the docks). These actions failed to trigger any support, either among the trade unions or among the populace. Political action, like the public campaign, appeared to be a thing of the past.

Yet the demonstrations and protests were not wholly in vain, for they did serve to channel and give a public echo to an anxiety running right through the social fabric.

The years of struggle also enabled certain individuals to gain and to consolidate a faith in combating abuses of all kinds, from the minor unauthorised pollution that the technocrats ignore to the way in which those same technocrats monopolise information. This is the role played by the eight anti-nuclear protesters of la Hague whom I mentioned earlier and who even today refuse to give up, remaining constantly on the alert for every threat of contamination, whether psychological or radioactive. They constitute a veritable public conscience, and all the local people whose will to protest is stifled by the lure of economic spin-offs, by fear of losing their jobs, or by an overwhelming feeling of impotence in the face of events, want to hang on to them at all costs: 'Ah, but there has to be some opposition to make sure that all the precautions get taken. Otherwise they'd do anything ... They'd do just as they liked up there!' Those eight men are the witnesses to and guarantors of the reality of the risk that so many deny. In a way they are the guardians of everybody's safety!

The failure of the environmental protest and the defeat of the political campaign left only the civic channel.

As a sop to Cherbourg's new Socialist MP, in 1981 a 'La Hague Committee of Information' was set up. Quadripartite in structure (with fifteen national and local elected representatives, five trade-union delegates, five leading scientists, and five representatives of environmental-protection organisations), it is chaired by the local MP and has its own budget and permanent administration in the shape of a scientific adviser. The committee's brief is 'to ascertain everything to do with the operation of the la Hague establishment and to gather all material information regarding its possible effects on the environment with a view to informing the local population thereof'.

The committee draws its finance from institutions at local and *département* level and above all from COGEMA. Consequently it is dependent, as regards both the studies it undertakes and the information available to it, on the goodwill of those institutions. This is the very point stressed by the present adviser when he told me:

> The committee 'informs'. However, it also needs to be informed. I usually hear about incidents that have occurred at the plant from the press or the anti-nuclear people! Fortunately, things are starting to change and the plant management now inform me more swiftly. The fact remains that I have no independent means of verification at my disposal, I only have those handed down by the official authorities. The committee gives its view in writing to the interested parties . . . If its reprimands have no effect, it can take action through the press. But before that we have to try every way we can to set up a strategy of dialogue between the institutions and the committee. That's what I'm trying to do.

Over the years the committee has acquired a measure of credibility. Its study of cancer deaths in Manche *département*[5] was regarded by many politicians with responsibility for health as interesting if rather too limited in terms of the period and the area covered. The committee suggested continuing the study by setting up a cancer monitoring unit for the department. The general council, however, refused to allocate funds for the work. With no budget of its own, the committee was unable to ignore this refusal and press ahead with the health-monitoring studies that it considered appropriate for the region.

The committee has yet to become the kind of independent forum for co-ordinated action and discussion that the public is looking for.

It took the Chernobyl disaster of April 1986 to give birth, in the Lower Normandy region, to an organisation that was completely independent of government. This was the 'Association for Controlling Radioactivity in the West' (*Association pour le contrôle de la radioactivité dans l'Ouest*, ACRO). It is a striking fact that the lesson of disaster appears to have stimulated a greater degree of awareness than ten years of militant action had managed to achieve.

Through this structure, which is independent of any kind of patronage, whether individual or collective, society has taken responsibility for itself.

The objects of the association are 'research and information concerning ionising radiation, whether natural or artificial, deliberate or accidental, and its short, medium, and long-term effects on human health and on the whole living ecosystem'. To perform these monitoring and measurement functions the association set up an analytical laboratory that carries out its own investigations as well as providing services to private individuals, local groups, nature-conservation organisations, and the like. The association's resources derive from subscriptions, grants, public money, street collections, and the sale of literature and services. ACRO has its own reliable methods of measurement, determined by independent scientists, and it makes its information available to the public as a matter of course. In this sense its role is complementary to if not in competition with (though in this case competition is an entirely positive thing) that of the Information Committee. Both bodies ought in future to become what la Hague still lacks, namely forums of consultation and reconciliation between society and the technocratic and bureaucratic authorities.

ACRO, in operation since the beginning of 1987, is at last beginning to become established. However, it can never hope to last except through the determination of individual citizens and local organisations. By the end of 1988, nine of the nineteen municipalities that make up la Hague had voted to give it a grant (those that refused did so on the grounds that COGEMA's own findings could, they felt, neither be doubted nor improved on, given that the plant had all the latest equipment). As for the district, loyal to its apolitical position on the question of nuclear safety, it has so far refused to subsidise ACRO. Nevertheless, in 1983–4 the same district council gave a grant of 20,000 francs to the standing Information Committee to help subsidise its study of cancer deaths in the *département*. No doubt the two institutions should not be seen as being on the same level. That, at any rate, is the view taken by the district in supporting the official committee that has the backing of COGEMA but refusing to help an organisation that is free and independent.

It is impossible to exaggerate the importance of this kind of independent organisation. ACRO represents the transition from one way of thinking to another. It stands for the desire and the determination of a section of the population of la Hague to break out of the circle of unreality, to rise above the fog of invariably alarming rumour that smothers this peninsula in thrall to the nuclear industry, and to escape at last from the perpetual gravitational pull of irony and black humour. They wish to cast aside these derisory weapons and strive, through genuine civic action, to become masters of their own fate.

It has taken them twenty years to get there. I believe it is a matter of urgency that all who occupy positions of political or social responsibility in the region should take note.

The silent years of the beginnings of the nuclearisation of la Hague gave way to the years of confrontation. Today, perhaps, we are seeing the dawn of the years of dialogue.

The nuclear industry has dramatically altered the political, geographical, and sociological landscape of the la Hague peninsula. As I have briefly indicated, certain lines are beginning to appear that serve to clarify the picture.

Some of these have to do with understanding la Hague today, a land that has been robbed of its identity by a high-risk industrial establishment, a territory that daily loses a little more of its space (constant companion since time immemorial) and experiences this as a disablement. What has emerged is an exploded society, stratified by fresh allegiances, seeking to preserve a sort of precarious status quo in order to maintain a semblance of equilibrium.

Understanding this has involved analysing the situation that obtained before the advent of the plant, certainly, but it has also involved grasping the profound historical, geographical, and cultural reasons why that process of industrialisation was able to take place.

On the side of history and psychological make-up there was the weight of centuries of obedience to the local notables, of submission in the face of orders from central government, and an overwhelming sense of the vanity of any kind of struggle against them. Hence the ease with which this mighty industrial invasion was ratified (you do not resist a force in motion because there is a good reason for things being the way they are and there is nothing you can do about it). Confronted with such fatalism, one catches oneself hoping that this society is trying to find itself again, seeking its unity, rediscovering its loyalties, and showing itself less shy about owning up to its fears and proclaiming its existence and its need to recover its identity through new methods of communication and new forms of awareness.

In getting to grips with this situation we have also become aware of a special relationship between the Hagars and their living-space, which they see and think of in terms of the shore and the sea, turning their backs on the hinterland where the plant has been built. Hence the temporary blindness that they manifest and that enables them to thrust these dangerous places away while at the same time creating (or re-creating) a natural environment to suit themselves.

These aspects of civilisation, together with others that I have touched on in the foregoing pages (the foundation myth suggesting that the destiny of this hybrid territory, this peninsula at the tip of a peninsula, is in fact one day to become an *island*), these features of the collective imagination, too often discounted in sociological studies, have had the effect of confirming, clarifying, but not, as I have been careful to remember, substituting for the historical facts and economic circumstances of the period.

Part II
The nuclear people

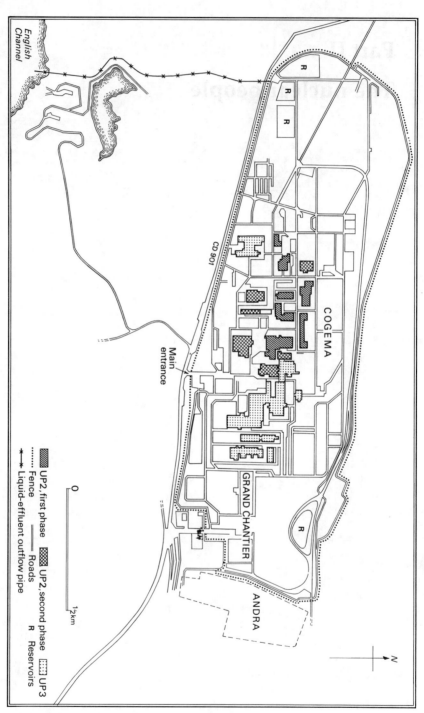

La Hague reprocessing plant

4 The nuclear site: an inventory of fixtures

It is time to turn our attention to the plant itself, the buildings of which are gradually taking over the plateau of la Hague, and to the men and women who converge on it day after day. Let us first try to find out who works there and what physical arrangements are in place on the site governing the organisation of this high-risk environment.

Talking in acronyms

Staff at the plant are either TDA, TNDA, or TNA. These initials denote the different categories of personnel and constitute the first 'words' you hear on entering the plant. Initials and acronyms abound on the site, peppering every conversation to the point of rendering it incomprehensible to the uninitiated. As well as categories of personnel, the various shops, the different departments, and the many boards and committees are all referred to in this way. Working at the plant involves familiarising yourself with a whole new language – a code, in effect, that allows those who belong to the plant not only to communicate with one another but to exclude 'outsiders'. From the outset there is an element of complicity between people who employ the acronyms and a corresponding exclusion of those who do not understand them. Not surprisingly, this hardly has the effect of facilitating communication between the nuclear people and the rest.

At the plant, initials and acronyms thus operate like the words of a language whose use is reserved for those who enter in and work *intra muros*. In fact, while workers may know 'whom' or 'what' the acronyms refer to, they very often do not know or have forgotten what they mean. Attempts to decipher what certain initials stand for will sometimes necessitate a prolonged inquiry, which may prove vain or may prove fruitful but invariably bespeaks a particular cast of mind. I spent a long time, for instance, trying to find out why the ventilated plastic outfit worn by workers who enter areas of heavy contamination is referred to as a 'shadock' suit. Was this yet another acronym? Or was it because people wearing them bore a resemblance to those little creatures mid way between men and animals, but with snouts and always equipped with pumps, made famous by a French television cartoon of the 1970s? More prosaically, had the airtight overalls been invented by a Mr Shadock? Most of the people I asked tended to go for the resemblance to strange creatures but without managing to make the connection with the cartoon, believing that the name had been invented by imaginative technicians. No one was able to give me the correct answer until one day I met the technician who had helped design the suit more than a decade before. He told me:

> To start with, it's written 'C.HA.DOC'. The C and the HA stand for 'combinaison Hague', because it was here at the plant that the suit was designed. Then the DOC got added because when you have the thing on you look like those cartoon characters, also the author's a local man, I mean from Normandy, which is why we thought of him.

People have forgotten the work of the men who designed this form of protective clothing, remembering only the extra-terrestrial, inhuman look assumed by technicians when they wear it. As often happens in the nuclear industry, imagination has got the better of what actually occurred.

Workers in the nuclear industry, then, are divided into those not assigned (*travailleurs non affectés*, TNA) to radioactive areas, workers not directly assigned (TNDA) to work in radioactive conditions but who may for one reason or another be so assigned on occasion, and workers directly assigned (TDA) to operations in areas where radio-activity is present. Personnel on the site are thus classified according to their degree of exposure to radiation, the point of course being to make sure that everyone receives the appropriate protection and medical supervision for his or her working conditions.

Yet behind these innocuous sets of initials, which vary by only one letter (accentuating the idea of equality, of all members of the plant being treated the same), there lies a hidden reality of divisions and hierarchies that influences the way in which the world of the nuclear industry is perceived, both by nuclear workers and in the surrounding society.

An initial split runs through the staff between those who work 'live' (*en actif*) (that is to say, in an ionising environment) and those who never enter radioactive areas. The second group includes the staffs of the administrative and social departments, members of management and the research departments, and those assigned to the various personnel departments. They are referred to by the first group (known as *les actifs*) as *stratifs*, a derogatory neologism that does indeed indicate a distinction between two spaces, two different modes of work. For the latter, the tranquil, normal rhythm of office life in premises shielded from any radioactivity; for the former, vigilance and shift work in shops that are never idle and are situated in areas where the atmosphere is liable to be contaminated.

The industrial section of the plant works round the clock, with up to five teams of between eight and nineteen persons (depending on the shop) relieving one another every eight hours. Of the workers attached to this section, some escape shift work, which leads to a further division between *les normaux*, whose operations conform to a normal timetable, and the shift workers (*les postés*), who work night and day, holidays included, following timetables that, being out of step with the usual rhythm of social or family life, generate very considerable psychological and social problems.

The lines between these groups are far from rigid. A technician may in the course of his career proceed from doing shift work to working normal hours. Members of management, no matter what category they belong to, come and go between the offices and the 'live' areas and between day work and shift work. However, because of their professional status, all members of management form a separate group, for which technicians use the generic term 'the hierarchy'.

But although these various labels (*stratifs/actifs*, *normaux/postés*, *la hiérarchie*) do actually denote distinct groups and indicate real differences between workers, the deepest divisions in this nuclear industry are those, paradoxically, that fall between members of the same category.

TDA employees include, among others, mechanical-intervention personnel, radioprotection personnel, and yet others with responsibility for decontamination.

The job of the mechanical-intervention group (*les mécaniciens*) is to repair and maintain all machinery and equipment. Such operators are required to work on instruments and machines situated in contaminated buildings and so difficult to get at that they sometimes have to invent new tools to carry out remote repairs on pieces of equipment that cannot be approached. Workers in this category are liable to very heavy exposure to radioactivity and have to wear and work in special clothing all the time. Despite these difficult working conditions and the exposed nature of their position, the engineers derive undoubted prestige from their technical skill and know-how. Among the other technicians they enjoy a very positive brand image, as it were. The proof surely lies in the fact that one of the few strikes to have broken out at the plant (in 1982, after it came under COGEMA control) took place in support of the engineers' demands for a reassessment of their professional status on account of the risks they ran in the course of their work.

Members of the Radioprotection Department have the job of measuring the radioactivity present in an area in which technicians need to operate, interpreting the measurements in terms of risk, determining a maximum period of intervention, and making sure the technician concerned does not exceed it. In order to carry out such measurements they enter ionised areas, exposing themselves to radiation and consequently taking steps to protect themselves. Their functions are various and of quite fundamental importance. They monitor the level of radioactivity in a shop and where necessary suggest measures to be taken to decontaminate it, deciding on and organising any interventions required. Their technical expertise has increased as new discoveries have led to improved ways of measuring radioactivity. Their increasingly complex methods are reliable and beyond dispute, and their skill is never called into question. Yet their role and position as intermediaries are not always entirely welcome. Obliged to explain the need for taking certain precautions, yet unable or unwilling to impose them, the radioprotection people are seen as part guardian angels, part police. Certain technicians, whether in radioprotection or on the other side, as it were, find this client relationship hard to take.

One of the few people I met who had left their jobs at the plant was a man who had belonged to the radioprotection department and had quit because he could not stand 'playing cop', as he put it. In a place where risks form the object of arbitration and are negotiated across the table between individuals, human relations take on some unsuspected resonances.

The third group, the decontaminators, comes into action whenever there is an incident involving radioactivity. They are the specialists at cleaning up contaminated equipment or premises. So they are always having to work in contaminated areas where they must wear special clothing. Their role is quite as indispensable as that of the mechanical operators so far as the smooth running of the plant is concerned, yet they are viewed in a wholly negative light. The jobs they are required to do are admittedly not 'high-tech', particularly as regards the basic operative who is expected simply to scrub contaminated areas with solvents, smash and throw away objects that cannot be salvaged, or attempt to suck up invisible radioactive dust with a vacuum-cleaner. These are banal, almost trivial occupations, but bear in mind the dangerous environment in which they are exercised and above all the derisory means available to modern technology when it comes to getting rid of a form of pollution that is invisible, inaudible, and has no smell. Jobs in decontamination consequently hold little attraction and are seen as conferring very little status.

'The decontaminators are the roadsweepers of the nuclear industry, the labourers, if you like!' 'Decontamination means sweeping up and doing the dishes,' another technician commented before adding: 'If I'm asked to do decontamination work, forget it, I'm not going in there. Monitoring in live areas, OK, because you're less exposed and the decontamination people have been through already and cleaned everything up.'

Understandably, this grade of personnel is among the least stable of all. Nobody lasts long, doing so dangerous a job with so little recognition from his or her workmates.

These obvious differences in the perception of jobs that, while not of course identical, are nevertheless all essential lead to different ways of experiencing the nuclear risk, of apprehending the danger. But what I should like to draw attention to here is a further perverse effect of these initials, namely the way in which, by imposing a superficial identity on jobs that are very different, they encourage people to ignore those differences or treat them in a cavalier fashion. This is in fact partly what the plant management does itself by entrusting the jobs that are under-valued, or difficult to accept mentally, to employees of outside firms operating under the direction of COGEMA staff. This subcontracted personnel is partly used for equipment maintenance work but is mainly employed on the basic tasks involved in radioprotection, decontamination, and general cleaning-up. In fact, there are virtually no COGEMA labourers as such. The unskilled labour at the plant is supplied by outside firms. To keep la Hague running COGEMA recruits mainly engineers, managers, and technicians who have passed their technical *baccalauréat* at least or who have the equivalent of an HND (*brevet de technicien supérieur*). Hence the comment of one trainee who had just been taken on by COGEMA and whom I asked about his job-to-be: 'I'm a decontaminator, but it won't be me doing the dirty work, it'll be contract workers. And I hope I shan't be there too long, either. I want to do radioprotection.'

This situation leads to an inevitable rift between COGEMA employees and those who, while working on the site in jobs that are often identical and performed in the same dangerous environment, enjoy neither the same advantages nor the same privileges, except as regards nuclear safety and medical protection. Moreover, between these two types of employee the air is full of accusations. The non-COGEMA people insist that the others are 'idle good-for-nothings, never in a hurry to get the job done because the cheque will be in the bank every month anyway, and they're well paid, too', while the COGEMA employees denounce the zeal of those who work for the outside firms, accusing them of trying to worm their way into COGEMA by showing off about how keen they are. Actually, there is some truth in this. Most of the stable jobs available in the region come from the plant, so that most of those looking for work would like to be taken on there. The subcontracting firms, aware of these aspirations, will occasionally exploit them. Some have the reputation of being virtual slave-drivers. To make themselves more competitive with the object of winning COGEMA contracts, they employ workers with few qualifications and little training for the jobs they are required to do. Moreover, they practise a sort of blackmail on their employees by holding up to them the chance of being taken on by COGEMA if they show themselves to be good at working in contaminated conditions and docile as regards agreeing to do so.

One trade unionist said this about a situation with which he was familiar:

> We had a set-to against that sort of thing, but we got nowhere. COGEMA said: we call in specialist firms because we can't do everything ourselves. So what happens? There are some outside firms that have been around for a long time and this is their business. I'm thinking of STMI,[1] they're an old firm, in fact they're part of the CEA group, their workers are well protected. Then there are other outfits that turn up, branches of cleaning companies that say they do decontamination. The fiercer the competition . . . the worse the workers are protected. Above all, a spell with an outside firm is presented as being an obligatory stepping-stone to getting into COGEMA. They say: 'we haven't got a job for you at the moment, but that firm over there may take you.' So the bloke goes along, signs up, and starts ruining his health. Because it's no joke, that kind of work. They work in vinyl suits with masks . . . It's a real drain on the organism, in fact they've worked out that some people lose between two and three kilos in an hour inside those suits.[2] Those people wear themselves out pretty quickly. Ten years, and they're medically unfit to go and work for COGEMA. It's a huge con trick, and people just aren't aware of it . . . All right, the contract people get the same medical follow-up and the same protection as COGEMA employees. But they're used more often than the others, and the monitoring may be less effective . . . And when they change firms their medical records don't always go with them! You see the sort of thing that can happen.

It is a fact that there are many stories in circulation about needless risks taken by employees of subcontractor firms: 'Radioprotection had said: you can work in there for three minutes . . . Well, I saw chaps trying to impress the boss by staying in there for five, six minutes.'

There are also known cases of outside workers who, having been involved in serious incidents, were then taken on by COGEMA. Others were not so lucky, if one can put it that way. 'In 1986 two chaps were said to have received between eleven and eighteen rems,[3] they were looked after . . . But they weren't taken on by COGEMA. For that you have to have received at least twenty-five rems . . . At that point there are statutory arrangements that come into effect.'

This division of nuclear workers between non-members and members of the plant undoubtedly poses very real economic and human problems. But we ought not to lose sight of another point, and that is the place occupied by the outside employees in the imaginations of COGEMA staff generally and even within the surrounding society. These people who do not form an integral part of the group but who come and go as temporary workers, taken on between campaigns (periods of operation) with little training and few qualifications, are often identified by the others as potential sources of trouble. If an incident occurred, no matter how minor or how serious, it would probably be their fault. That, at any rate, was the answer people gave when I mentioned the possibility of incidents on the site. The wife of one plant technician put it like this:

> With proper workers, like my husband, there's nothing to fear. What frightens me is carelessness by people who are unfamiliar with the place, who are hired on a temporary basis during the holidays or on free evenings or at night, shifts that drink and don't see the alarms and get up to all sorts of things!

This class of workers, people who revolve around the plant without really being part of it, constitute an ideal 'scapegoat' and one that it is difficult, in this context, not to exploit as such. The more so since in this vast establishment, which even its employees admit is 'not on a human scale any more', each group can easily find another, a 'them' group of which it forms no part, to blame for any trouble that may occur.

The latent opposition that exists currently among plant personnel between the 'older generations' and the 'youngsters' recently taken on at UP3 might, in the short term, provide a magnet for the accusation of 'troublemaker' in the sense of someone who causes incidents:

> It's customary to say that there are three generations at the plant. The first goes up to 1976, knew the CEA, built the plant, and got it started. The second began in 1977, when a lot of people were taken on at the time the HAO shops were built. The third generation is the people recruited since 1981. There's no real problem between the first and second. The veterans taught us our jobs, we went through the same sorts of experience. The problem is all these young people in a new plant, unfamiliar with the set-up. They need to be trained, but since they all have diplomas they're not necessarily going to listen to their elders!

Following changes in the law regarding the employment of women in high-risk sectors in 1986,[4] women entered the plant in various laboratories and on production or monitoring teams. This female invasion of a dangerous industrial environment hitherto entirely dominated by men called for some adjustment. 'The advent of women did shift people's way of thinking, in fact . . . You'd have heard the union people going on against women being allowed in . . . Some said it was a deliberate move to break up the male shift teams . . .' What is the betting that, if the number of female technicians increases (there were nineteen of them working 'live' at the time of this study), they will constitute a perfect 'scapegoat' group?

So these harmless sets of initials, these apparently monolithic acronyms, conceal a world that is riddled with splits and ruptures.

'Going on-limits'

To ensure that personnel are fully protected against radioactivity, the whole of the la Hague plant is organised in 'zones'. An initial division splits the site into non-regulated and monitored areas, the latter being subdivided into controlled zones of varying sizes.

The non-regulated zone comprises the areas and buildings where personnel are unlikely to receive radiation doses above 1.5 rems per annum. Staff employed here wear their ordinary clothes. The zone comprises the offices, canteens, trade union and social premises, and leisure and recreation areas. There are no signs or alarms, whether sirens or flashing lights, to indicate to those who come there daily that they are on a nuclear site, with perhaps the sole exception of the breathing masks in a glass case on one of the corridor walls, each mask bearing a name corresponding to those on the little labels on the doors that line that corridor. Clearly, everyone has his or her survival mask in case an incident occurs.

Nevertheless, as employees in the non-regulated zone move about the site they pass buildings painted in the colours of the landscape with blind façades through which no smell or light or sound escapes that might disturb them. Nor do they ever see smoke escaping from the tall chimneys. Outside they are surrounded by the reassuringly familiar sounds of a building site as vehicles criss-cross the plateau in all directions and the wind whistles ceaselessly through the metal skeletons of the cranes. Understandably, in the circumstances, those who work in the non-regulated zone state that they feel fine there and pay no heed to the danger surrounding them: 'The risk ... I never think about it,' one secretary said, 'otherwise I shouldn't be here, and I moved heaven and earth to get here.'

The situation is different in the monitored zone and inside the three controlled zones. The moment you enter the so-called '600' monitored zone you become a different person. You are now a proper nuclear worker. You remove your street clothes, don the universal garb (special footwear, white jacket and trousers for men, blue for women, and a green coat for visitors), and equip yourself with film badges to measure ambient radioactivity. In this '600' zone, discharges of dose equivalents should average fewer than 2.5 millirems per hour. It is the zone of normal working in the main research units and laboratories of the plant. Beyond that you come to the '700' and '800' controlled zones, which include the various fuel-reprocessing shops. Here people can normally work in white suits except in the event of breaches of containment, leaks, or particular tasks, when special vinyl suits are worn. In these zones dose discharges are of the order of 2.5 to 10 millirems per hour. Lastly, in the '900' zone, where discharges of dose equivalents are 10 millirems per hour[5] and upwards, all activity is banned as a rule, and on the exceptional occasions when it is necessary for staff to enter the area they wear specially adapted space suits.

In the shops these three zones are marked out in such a way that it is impossible to pass from one to another without taking essential precautions. A person must learn a whole language of signs and symbols (notice-boards, colours, figures) encountered during the course of a day's work. Knowledge of that language is of vital importance.

'Working on-limits' or 'going on-limits' (*travailler en zone, aller en zone*) are typical phrases used by the nuclear worker, and it is important to bear in mind the many constraints he is under by virtue of the tasks he performs in contaminated surroundings or the radioactive products he handles.

The zones are always separated from one another physically, though they may exist side-by-side within the same building. A shop, for example, may be divided into a sector '700' peripheral area, where the technician spends most of his time, and a core, corner, or basement (depending on the operation involved) belonging to sectors '800' or '900'. Protective walls vary according to the type of radiation (alpha, beta, or gamma) given off by the materials or components against which workers need protection.

In the plutonium-processing building (plutonium being a source of alpha radiation, which a sheet of paper will block but which is extremely dangerous once it gets inside the body) or in the laboratories, technicians work with the protection of 'glove boxes', small enclosures with plexiglass walls inside which manual operations can be carried out with the aid of plastic sleeves fitted with gloves that are attached to the wall. For certain operations it may be necessary to don one or more extra pairs of gloves before using the boxes with the gloves already fitted. The cutting-up of uranium rods (uranium is an element that emits very high-energy gamma radiation) is done with the aid of remote manipulators behind concrete walls and lead glass partitions. When removing spent fuel rods from their steel containers and placing them in baskets, the operator works on a bridge above a tank in which both containers and baskets are immersed, the water serving to shield him from the radioactivity being given off.

These various forms of protection placed between the operator and the radiation source allow him to remain in a '700' zone while working, with the aid of special tools, in highly radioactive areas.

Occasionally, however, technicians are required to intervene directly in areas where there have been breaches of containment or leaks in order to carry out repairs, do cleaning work, or replace parts (a length of tubing, a screw, a light bulb). Then they have to wear a special outfit made of pink vinyl.

The whole outfit consists of a white cotton boiler suit over which the operator wears a vinyl jacket and trousers. His feet are encased in flexible shoes with three pairs of cotton overboots and one of vinyl, his hands in three pairs of gloves sealed to the jacket with tarlatan. On his head he wears a cap, then a hood, then the hood of the vinyl jacket. Lastly, he wears a breathing mask to protect his respiratory tracts. For operations in particularly contaminated areas, the technician tops all this with a flexible 'space suit' of white vinyl with a tube supplying him with fresh air. This is the notorious 'shadock' suit.

The wearing of such an outfit has to be learned, and this can only be done with the help of a 'veteran', who will show the novice the 'tricks of the trade': how to prepare the strips of tarlatan, folding back an end to make it easier to unpeel them, putting the overboots on first with the cotton trousers outside them, then the vinyl trousers with the vinyl overboots inside, and so on. It is very warm inside the outfit, you are soon bathed in perspiration, the glass of the mask fogs up, your heart beats faster, pounding in your ears, you feel as if you are suffocating, and there is only one thing you want to do, at least the first time you don the outfit, and that is to take it all off. After a while, I was told, 'you get used to it'. 'When you know what you're doing it takes ten minutes to put it all on, three pairs of overboots, three pairs of gloves, the mask, the hood . . . You know what you're doing, you're quick, you're used to it. When a youngster comes along we take him in hand.'

The same strict ceremonial governs the undressing part. In the first compartment you remove one vinyl 'skin', starting with one foot, which you then, endeavouring to keep your balance, place in the second compartment. Then you go on to the second foot, the trousers, the jacket, the first pair of gloves, and so on. The important thing is, so far as possible, 'not to spread the contamination', whence the different undressing compartments, each with its bin into which the worker, as he strips off each layer, throws the plastic skins that formerly encased him. All these items of clothing are subsequently collected, sorted, placed in steel containers, and carted off to ANDRA. Each operation in this waste-reprocessing plant creates further waste; the cycle of waste creation is endless.

Once the clothing has been removed, the worker must be

monitored. He thrusts his hands and feet into appliances fitted with a kind of photo-electric cell that triggers a sound or light signal of greater or lesser intensity depending on the level of radioactivity the operator is carrying. A similar, portable device monitors any radioactivity he may have received on his hair or on his body. These checks are carried out every time a worker emerges from one of the controlled zones; each time a person passes between sectors with different levels of radioactivity, staff carry out a meticulous inspection of his clothing and his body for any trace of contamination.

Only people who share the experience can fully appreciate the strain imposed by such working conditions. How can a person convey this daily familiarity with danger and fear to anyone other than his shift mates? 'As far as many of us are concerned, you just daren't open up . . . I've seen that at the plant: the ones who are scared will only talk about their fear if you'll talk about yours. And anyway, for a lot of people, admitting you're scared is as good as saying you're chicken, you're not a man.'

In these few words a former employee of the plant encapsulated both the impossibility of communicating and the resultant feeling of moral unease. This makes it simpler to understand the gulf that exists among members of the staff of the plant between those who work 'on-limits' and those who never enter controlled zones. They form two groups that, though they may rub shoulders, live in two different worlds. The same phenomenon accounts for the silence observed by nuclear workers in the company of their families and friends, to whom they will say nothing about what they do or about what goes on 'up there'.

One also hears tell (and the discomfort of working conditions in a nuclear environment makes it understandable that such stories should circulate) of operators who, coming 'off-limits' quite confident that they are not contaminated, and in any case in a hurry, neglect to carry out the proper checks on themselves.

> So the bloke, from what I heard, it was knocking-off time and he didn't want to miss his bus, didn't check himself but went home with it on him. He came back next day, checked himself, and found he was contaminated . . . They checked all his street clothing, they went round to his place and found it everywhere he'd been, on his sheets, on his toothbrush . . . I mean, everywhere . . . They threw everything away or cleaned it all at the plant, but you should have seen the state his clothes came out in.

However, the training received by all employees is designed to make it impossible for such things to happen.

5 Learning the nuclear ropes

The special nature of work in a nuclear environment and the activities peculiar to the la Hague plant form the subject of a training course that is compulsory for everyone who is required to work on the site for longer than a month, whether employed directly by the plant or by one of the outside firms. Other specialised courses are available to COGEMA staff during their careers or when they are first taken on, because the very special nature of the operations involved in reprocessing means that it is impossible to use technicians coming straight from the state educational system. It is therefore essential, once staff with a particular level of technical qualification have been recruited, that they be given specific training. Hence the numerous training cycles that staff at the plant may pursue.

However, the one that is actually called the *stage de formation* or 'training course' is the only one that, at least so far as its theoretical content is concerned, is followed by all personnel present on the site, with the sole exception of management engineers, who do not require any additional instruction. The training course thus constitutes an apprenticeship in nuclear safety and in the industrial operations performed on the site that is shared by all administrative and skilled personnel, a presentation of a form of knowledge concerning matters nuclear that they all have in common. Right from this initial contact, however, technicians and administrative staff are segregated. Each course in fact consists of a dozen or so persons set by affinity of occupation and technical grade. A division is established between the two groups from the outset, just as a gulf is fixed between those who work 'live' and the rest, because the session is split into two parts. The first, extending over two days, is termed 'theoretical' and is attended by all trainees; the second, which lasts for a further two days, is termed 'practical' and includes only those workers who are required to operate in controlled zones.

Information as formation

The training course is held at the plant itself, in special premises set aside for the purpose. It is taken by an instructor who says neither where he has worked nor in which sector of nuclear operations. Consequently, you have no means of knowing exactly whom you are dealing with except a teacher whose job it is to teach you what you should know about *le nucléaire*. My first impression on attending this course was that, pedagogically speaking, we were treated like school-children. A booklet was handed out, which we were urged to read closely. The instructor made particular reference to the level of technical knowledge that his hearers were assumed to possess, thus setting them up in competition with one another. Then, when he had finished explaining something, he asked exam-type questions to which he expected a group oral response enabling him to ascertain whether he had been fully understood. At no time did the instructor take any account of the individual trainees themselves, of the jobs they would be doing or were already doing, or of their personal back-grounds. No attempt was made to observe behaviour or recognise emotions. In other words, sessions took the form not of exchanges but simply of lessons that had to be learned.

Not surprisingly, in the circumstances, few questions were asked and little additional explanation was called for. Just occasionally, however, a thought touching on one or another aspect of nuclear energy would float to the surface:

What's the risk of someone not checking himself when he comes off-limits? Does that ever happen?

So you come off-limits the minute you begin to feel tired, right?

If a person dies . . . is the cemetery radioactive? In fact, don't they say Marie Curie was buried in a lead coffin?

The long-term effects of radiation . . . Is anything known about that?

Could Chernobyl happen in France – is that possible?

Obliquely, using humour, and speaking in terms of 'other people' or 'somewhere else', trainees gave expression to a latent anxiety that had to do with the overt or surreptitious fear of death that haunts this place.

Such questions never received a straight answer but were always replied to indirectly, using for comparison facts that, while arising out of everyday life, do not spontaneously spring to mind, the object being to place people's fear in perspective and so loosen its grip: 'The mineral water you drink is much more radioactive . . . The population of Sweden is far more exposed to natural radioactivity . . . than people working in a nuclear power station . . . Our reactors are safer than the Russian ones. Also, their technicians are untrained!'

The whole course is dominated by such reassuring, ironical, distanced language. Possibly the aim is to create a sort of habituation to fear, to alleviate the beginner's misgivings. A former instructor implicitly confirmed this:

> With people who had just been taken on I was aware of a certain apprehension, a blue funk, frankly, about nuclear energy. Then once they're in . . . it goes away. They feel that people had given them an exaggerated idea of the risks. They get into a routine, and from hearing so often that in the nuclear industry every precaution is taken they end up believing it.

The effects of this language, which tends to relativise everything and seeks to remove all fear, go very much further than that. They allow the nuclear worker to adopt a casual attitude towards safety 'because nothing ever goes wrong here'.

Moreover, the feeling of confidence instilled by the instructor's remarks was reinforced by the recital, in stirring tones, of the history of France's nuclear policy and the place of the la Hague plant in the overall scheme of things. He went through the various stages of construction of the different shops, up to and including UP3, which will be the most modern reprocessing plant in the world and for which the most advanced solutions known to robotics and information technology are currently being perfected and implemented. There was plenty here to give people the feeling that they were working in a high-tech industry. And there was a dash of national pride thrown in. In reprocessing, trainees were told, we are not only the best but also the cheapest. Hence all the foreign contracts that France has won in this field and that are financing the construction of UP3 100 per cent.

At no point was the local history of the plant recounted, any more than people dwelt on its pioneering past and on the generation that developed it.

> Because if this plant works [one ex-employee recalls] it's thanks to us. Other countries have either stopped reprocessing or have run into all kinds of trouble. We saw to it that worker safety is guaranteed and that dose levels are lower than in other places . . . We fought for all that. Now they're trying to give our whole generation the push.

Clearly it is not that kind of history that they wish to pass on to newcomers but the kind that recounts the legendary epic of the French nuclear industry, in which reprocessing constitutes a glorious chapter. To tell it, COGEMA relies on film. A modern medium of expression and as such suited to a setting dedicated to technology, film is also, of course, a medium that lends itself to manipulation.

The short films that punctuate the training sessions like so many cadenzas in glorification of nuclear energy all revolve around two concerns, which are kept separate or blended together, depending on the length or purpose of the film. Those concerns are on the one hand to *tell the story* of man's conquest of nuclear energy and on the other to *demonstrate*, by means of mock-ups or suitable diagrams, the safety of the buildings and equipment used in the nuclear industry. In other words, COGEMA's films illustrate man's total mastery of this fabulous natural source of energy. Breaks of rhythm in the way the images unfold, changes of voice, switches from black-and-white to colour, and modifications in the sound track are clues indicating a shift from one concern to the other. Interestingly, it is always (at least in the films I got to see) a female voice that provides the commentary in passages relating to safety or to incidents and a male voice that narrates the nuclear epic. Accident and traumatism are allotted to the female world, but so is the ability to reassure and heal. The male world gets technical expertise, the power to tame nature, mankind's mastery of the elements. These short films, produced for training purposes, perpetuate the stereotypes of our society.

Be that as it may, if the function of these films is to win the viewer round to the type of work presented in them, they perform it to perfection, judging by the complete absence of questions or comments of any kind after each showing.

How and why is reprocessing done?

France has made a decision to take on the whole cycle of nuclear-energy production. That includes the extraction and enrichment of the ore, the production of energy in nuclear reactors, and finally the reprocessing of the spent fuel. This last phase of the cycle appears to be necessary for two main reasons. Firstly, reprocessing makes it possible to separate the different elements contained in the fuel and consequently to recover the uranium, giving France a measure of self-sufficiency as far as the supply of that mineral is concerned. Secondly, it provides the plutonium formerly needed for the manufacture of thermonuclear weapons and now used either for fuel in the fast-breeder reactors that France may eventually build or to manufacture MOX, the new fuel for pressurised-water reactors.

The la Hague plant thus reprocesses the spent fuel from nuclear power stations equipped with PWRs. Once every three years such reactors are unloaded and the uranium rods that constitute their fuel are placed in a 'pond' (*piscine* in French, a word that usually means 'swimming-pool') for about a year to allow their radioactivity to diminish. The spent fuel rods cannot be transported immediately. It is only after this period has elapsed that they are placed in flasks (grandly referred to as *châteaux* in French), huge containers measuring between four and six metres in length and weighing between 80 and 110 (metric) tons, with thick steel walls fitted with steel fins on the outside to allow the air to circulate more efficiently. The flasks are brought by train to Valognes or by boat to Cherbourg. From there they are taken by road to the la Hague plant, possibly under heavy police escort when demonstrations by environmentalists disturb or rather used to disturb the arrival of shipments.

Immediately on arrival at the plant the fuel is removed from the flasks and once again placed (this time for three years) in a *piscine* where the water is kept under constant refrigeration and where the rods lose a further fraction of their radioactivity. 'First the life of Reilly [*vie de château*], then they get to lounge in the pool for a while . . . ', one lecturer remarked, evoking, no doubt unwittingly, the wealth of precautions that surround this substance so special as to invite the use of words normally reserved for human beings. Much of the symbolism assigned to nuclear energy stems from the kind of language in which it is enshrined.

Following this period of storage comes the operation known as '*shearing*', when the fuel rods and their protective sheaths or 'cans' are cut into short lengths. Cans and spent fuel are then separated, after which the former are rinsed and stockpiled and the latter enters the *dissolution* phase. The material is completely dissolved in boiling concentrated nitric acid. In the process, certain volatile gases are given off (krypton 85, xenon 133, and iodine 131, for example). All danger-ous in varying degrees, these need to be 'trapped' before being released into the atmosphere. What is left is a complicated solution of uranium nitrate, plutonium nitrate, transuranic elements, and fission products,[1] the constituents of which then need to be extracted. The last two ingredients are transferred to a special treatment shop. As for the uranium and plutonium solutions, they undergo first separation and then *purification*. The uranium is concentrated in nitrate form before being dispatched in metal drums to refining and conversion plants situated in the Rhône valley near Montélimar. The plutonium is purified and turned into oxide form for use in fast-breeder reactors. It, too, is dispatched in metal containers. It remains to *treat* and *condition* the fission products, transuranic elements, and other waste resulting from the preceding stages. The fission products contain virtually all the radioactivity of the spent fuel that entered the plant. Some of them, for example the isotopes of caesium and strontium, have a very high level of radioactivity (still 300,000 curies per ton ten years after removal from the reactor) but a short half-life[2] (around thirty years). Others, such as neptunium and americium, have lower levels of radioactivity (10,000 curies per ton after ten years) but extremely long half-lives (more than two million years in the case of neptunium 237).

Currently these so-called 'high-level' waste products are stockpiled on site in stainless-steel drums that are lowered into shafts dug beneath the plant and kept constantly ventilated. Low-level radioactive solutions are sent to the liquid-effluent treatment station, where as many radioactive products as possible are removed (by filtration, various chemical reactions, evaporation, and other processes). A small amount of radioactivity is always left in the water that is eventually discharged into the sea through the long pipe that starts from the plant and ends five kilometres out in the 'raz Blanchard', the tidal race that rounds the tip of the peninsula. 'It's let out when the tide turns. That way the stuff (*la sauce*) gets carried right off.'

Gaseous effluent is discharged from the tall chimneys that dominate the site. This is done when the wind is blowing at between eight and twelve knots and will disperse the gases more readily.

Finally, the residue that has been filtered out of the low-level waste, the rubbish from the various handling processes performed in the shops and laboratories, and the objects and plastic clothing used and contaminated during operations in ionising areas are placed in special containers and sent 'next-door' to ANDRA.

The cycle of the reprocessing of radioactive waste is completed by the release into the environment and the stockpiling at various sites and in various forms of other radioactive waste.

The languages of the nuclear industry

Reprocessing is probably the most delicate and dangerous phase in the nuclear fuel cycle: it involves a large number of complex operations, and the material being handled is enormously radioactive. These notions of skill on the one hand and danger on the other, while very much bound up with the reprocessing cycle, are never mentioned by the instructor taking the training course. On the contrary, the things he stresses are the *safety* and the *simplicity* of each phase. For instance, the flasks in which the spent fuel is shipped are designed to withstand every kind of accident (a film is shown to back up this claim), and the storage ponds are built to take an earthquake measuring seven on the Richter scale.

He also made the point that the fission products are stored in deep wells under constant refrigeration, needing only an electricity supply. It so happens that in 1980 a fire destroyed both the regular circuit and the emergency circuit and generators had to be brought in from outside. 'There was a scare, but everything was brought under control and it couldn't happen again because the electrical circuits have been duplicated . . . ' This is the only incident on the site to which reference was made during the whole of the training course that I attended. No other one was mentioned, nor did the trainees ask any questions on the subject.

Incidentally, during the second part of the course, when the instructor was talking about the neutron-detecting devices used in the shops where plutonium is handled, a point was made concerning that element's particularly low critical mass,[3] whence the need to store it in very small quantities. No doubt alarmed, one trainee asked anxiously: 'Do you have evacuation drills on the site?' Answer: 'Yes, from time to time, but in the buildings all you have to do is follow the arrows to the muster stations indicated.'

So far as both parties were concerned, the instructor and the trainees, it was just as if the subject of 'an accident on the site' should not or could not be tackled head-on. Not that there have been none to deplore in the twenty or more years during which the plant has been in operation: there have in fact been two or three significant accidents in the sense that they affected plant personnel as well as posing a threat to the environment. But in this kind of industrial establishment there are always risks of potentially major accidents occurring. Indeed, they are duly listed and itemised, the better to guard against them. And in any case the chance of such disasters actually happening is wholly discounted by the technicians.

> There couldn't be a major accident here. There are two places where it might happen. At PU [the plutonium building] there's a risk of critical mass, but the building is continually being redesigned to improve safety, and they're careful about the kinds and quantities of plutonium stockpiled there. Then there are the fission products in tanks where the air has to be kept moving the whole time. But you've got twenty hours before it becomes dangerous ... So as we saw with the generator fire there'll always be a way of finding a replacement in time ...

It was as if the contingency of these known and allegedly controlled risks could not be commented on, just as there was no mention during my training course of incidents that had occurred on the site. It would be tantamount to acknowledging the reality of the risk, and that is something no one wants to know about. Consequently, no one here possesses the words or the language to express or articulate his fears and anxieties regarding the risks he runs. Everyone keeps quiet and says nothing about what might happen at the plant.

There was some talk, during the course, of nuclear catastrophe, but always of the one that occurred somewhere else, a long way off, namely at Chernobyl. The trainees did request information about this foreign disaster, and the instructor had to spend some time dealing with it. He explained, for example, that it was made possible by the age of the Soviet nuclear installations and by the lack of specialist

training among the staff manning them ('they're just electricians!').
France's nuclear installations looked utterly reliable in comparison.

The nuclear industry is well aware of this 'Chernobyl effect'. 'Since
Chernobyl they [French engineers] have been able to say that they're
better than the Russians, and anyway the fact that Chernobyl was not
such an enormous disaster makes nuclear incidents less special.
Chernobyl suited a lot of people down to the ground.' There is a
certain overlap here, actually, between the interests of the technocrats
and the psychology of the employees, for Chernobyl offers the latter,
too, a pretext for talking about accidents without actually mentioning
those that might come to threaten them here.

So the various phases of the reprocessing operation offer every
guarantee of safety. Above all, they are *simple* to perform. The work is
always represented as easy, straightforward, and involving very little
danger, so long as a person takes a bit of care. In fact, all the pedagogic
metaphors employed to explain what happens at each stage are taken
from the vocabulary of the *domestic sphere*, and specifically from the
female side of the domestic sphere, namely *cookery* and *housework*.

The reactor is like a pressure-cooker . . .

Get too close and you'll be like a boiled leek.

There's the soup, the juice, and afterwards we discharge the gravy . . .

The plant's as simple as a dairy, except that you're dealing with radioactive
products . . .

Things are dunked in a tank of water . . . like on a farmyard . . . It's no more
complicated than your good wife at work in her kitchen!

You have to leave your place clean . . . not make a mess . . .

When you're undressing you must put your feet in the right place so as not
to make a mess . . . Throw your things in the drum provided and don't
leave anything lying around . . .

The tenuous, subtle balance that it is felt necessary to maintain
when introducing the jobs that punctuate the reprocessing cycle, a
balance between their relative simplicity on the one hand and their
extreme dangerousness on the other, tends (at least, it did during the
training course) to highlight the former aspect at the expense of the
latter. The scientific, technical language (intended to give an impression of knowledge and competence) to which I was treated during
conversations off the site and that I found used in the scientific
publications, too, while it was also employed on the training course,
was in part thwarted by other linguistic practices that leaned towards
the domestic. The transfer of knowledge was in this case achieved

with the aid of a banal, commonplace vocabulary that had the effect of trivialising any danger.

But as a result of euphemising the risk and treating it almost nonchalantly, saying things like: 'They take every precaution here. In the nuclear industry you're monitored, traced ... It's not like in chemicals! Here you're watched like a pan of milk on the stove!' The worker forgets his anxieties and represses his fear to the point, sometimes, of not taking due care. 'People under-estimate the risks so seriously and are so much not traumatised by the doses they receive that they have the feeling of getting into a routine, as a result of which they start making silly mistakes ... '

And at the same time as the risks are played down in this way, the jobs that these men do are repeatedly likened to women's work ('It's no more complicated here than in a dairy').

And then there is the remark that a well-known trade unionist, André Bergeron of Force Ouvrière, came out with when he visited the site (the sentence remains engraved in the memories of all la Hague workers): 'It's as spotless as a laundry, your plant!'

A metaphor can sometimes be out of place. Obviously technicians are not going to think much of being bracketed with cooks, laundry-women, and dairymaids!

Risk and protection

On top of these collective risks associated with the various stages of the reprocessing cycle, everyone who works in a controlled zone is exposed to two particular types of danger arising from radioactivity.

One is *contamination*, which results from invisible dust particles given off by radioactive substances coming into contact with a person and possibly affecting that person either externally or internally. The other is *irradiation*, due to the equally invisible rays given off by nuclear substances and capable of affecting the human body.

Radioactive dust particles, once they have settled, proceed to give off radiation internally or externally. When a person emerges from the radioactive beam, however, irradiation ceases (except that certain types of radiation are capable of penetrating the human body and becoming contaminative in their effect).

These two ways of being affected by radioactivity are perceived very differently by workers in the nuclear industry, although biologically they lead to the same result, namely that in both cases radioactivity penetrates and spreads through the human organism.

During the training course these risks associated with handling nuclear substances were defined and briefly explained, but they were then set in the context of such a wealth of definitions and of comments

so diverse in terms of both word and image that it seemed to me that
the trainees forgot all about the dangers they faced or at least did not
strive to gain any precise awareness of them, remembering only the
scientific, historical, even anecdotal aspects of *le nucléaire*.

For instance, after listing the dangers to which a person was
exposed on the site, the instructor immediately moved on to defining
the various types of radiation given off by radioactive substances,
because it is a fact that alpha, beta, and gamma rays all produce
different kinds of biological effect. There followed a passage on the
half-lives of nuclear substances. The one they are particularly wary of
at la Hague is plutonium 239, which has a half-life of 24,000 years and
which also emits alpha rays, making it hard to detect because a thin
film of water or a sheet of paper are sufficient to block this type of
radiation. In the same session we were told that a body is radioactive
when emitting radiation measured in terms of the number of disintegrations per second, one disintegration being equal to one becquerel
(Bq), not to be confused with the rem, the other unit of measurement
that we have already come across and that is used to define and assess
the 'quality' of the radioactive doses absorbed by a person, whether
naturally or by contrivance.

Barring accidents, no one at the la Hague plant is subjected to heavy
doses of radioactivity. The most exposed worker receives no more
than 5 rems a year, which constitutes his 'entitlement' (*à laquelle il a
droit*), as he will say and as is said generally. Moreover, so far as
possible this 'permitted dose' is rationed out over the course of a year's
work. Indeed, it is calculated in terms of hours worked, so that an
operator subjected to 5 rems a year who works 2,000 hours is 'entitled'
to 20 millirems a day or 400 millirems a month. If for any reason he
should happen to receive more than the permitted daily dose he is 'put
out to grass' (*mis au vert*) for as long as is necessary to bring him down
to the proper level.[4]

So everyone here has to keep a check on the doses he receives
during the year. To this end every operator who is required to work
on-limits is issued with special dosemeters known as 'film badges',
which contain a piece of photographic film that is sensitive to ambient
radioactivity. He pins one on his chest and wears the other on his
wrist. The pieces of film are developed every month and the results
given to the operator. If he is required to enter a more radioactive
sector than the one he normally works in, he must carry more sensitive
measuring instruments that above all give an instant reading. One
such is the pen-dosemeter, which can be clipped on the chest and
which measures the dose accumulated over a given period, since it can
be set to go off when the permitted period of intervention has elapsed.
After each use or at the end of a certain period, depending on how the

pen-dosemeter is being used, the counter is reset at zero. The operator may also use a detector with an alarm, which is a dosemeter the size of a cigarette packet that goes off when the period of exposure is exceeded, or he may equip himself with tiny pellets of lithium fluoride (referred to in French as *fli*), which he sticks on his fingertips or on the tools he is using and which also give an instant reading of ambient radioactivity when placed beneath the appropriate instrument.

Film badges are personal, of course, and have the user's name written on them. The other alarms, which anyone may use, are reset at zero after each outing. In other words, each person assumes responsibility for his own protection. He must check the measuring instruments constantly, make sure he has the right alarms for the sector he intends to enter, and check himself every time he comes off-limits.

However, when an operator has to do something in an area where there is a breach of containment or in the highly radioactive '900' zone, he is looked after by members of the Radioprotection Department. They determine both the period of intervention and the clothing to be worn. In a sense, that operator's safety is guaranteed by others. This daily switching between auto- and allo-protection does pose certain problems of adjustment between radioprotectionists and technical operators. And in nuclear establishments the debate between the adherents of self-protection and those who advocate 'piloting' (when experts assume responsibility for protecting the operator) is anything but resolved.

> The EDF people say we [COGEMA's Radioprotection Department] have completely missed the point . . . that we've transformed the role of radioprotection into one of policing and in so doing have taken away the individual's sense of responsibility . . . We've removed his motivation . . . undermined his perception of reality. They make radioprotection an integral part of the job. It's the man doing the job who sees to his own safety. That involves a great deal. It means he takes his own radiation measurements and his own contamination samples, analyses them, and organises his work accordingly. And on top of that he has to get his work done. They make a lot of the fact that they trust people, give them responsibility. It's all very well in theory, but in practice . . . It's like on the roads. People have been told that cars are dangerous things, but it's obvious that fear of the police is the only thing that makes them slow down . . . Ought we to review our principle? Things go wrong at EDF. My own view is that a man cannot do the job that we do on a full-time basis and also do electronics . . . mechanical engineering . . . maintenance work . . . It's better he should be assisted, piloted by experts like ourselves, but there's another side to it, and that is that people start leaving it all to us . . . It's a job to decide between the two approaches.

Whichever approach to safety a man advocates, the fact remains that in this dangerous world he is constantly equipped with instruments that enable him to assess at any given moment the risks he is running in the particular place where he is working. He is further surrounded by devices to measure ambient radioactivity that give off sound signals in case of emergency. His daily life is thus marked out by sentries ready to warn him of danger, and he must remain alert to them. But in a place like this, where the danger is invisible and may be perceived only through the medium of artificial aids (counters, alarms, and bits of film providing the only direct evidence of this thing called 'radioactivity'), the big question that arises, at least so far as I as a lay person am concerned, is that of people's confidence in these devices, the credence they place in them. That seems to me to be crucial. Yet during the training course not one person touched on the problem. Later I understood why. There is in fact a symbolic and metaphorical process of transformation involved, whereby these objects, from being mere instruments for measuring radioactivity, become actual means of protection. This being so, there is little point in inquiring about their reliability: it is an article of faith.

In certain circumstances these mechanical sentries are backed up by an expert technician who watches over the worker's safety and with whom the worker must form an understanding. Thus each technician daily forms the focus of a complex arrangement calling for great vigilance and as great a degree of flexibility. This part of the course, devoted to the risks present in a nuclear environment, struck me as particularly dense. It was abundantly illustrated (with a film, slides, and presentations of measuring equipment), yet it did not appear to arouse any greater degree of interest among the trainees than the other parts. They took no notes and asked very few questions, apart from: 'Do you get the same money when you're put out to grass?'

Is that how people experience constant risk? Or does fear of unemployment (the question was asked by a 'non-COGEMA' employee) override every defence?

First aid

Despite all these precautions, incidents of irradiation or contamination are an almost daily occurrence on the site. The victims are then taken in hand by the plant's Medical Department. A nurse member of that department came along at the end of the first part of the course to explain how it looks after people.

Beyond a doubt, this session was the liveliest of the whole course. The audience asked questions, talked about how they had got the job, and recounted accidents involving radioactivity of which they had heard tell. All at once it was as if the group was taking shape, reacting as a group in order to ask for more information, demand further explanations, criticise the constraints to which everyone here must submit.

Was this because of the nurse-instructor himself, a jovial, straight-forward sort of man who gained his audience's confidence as soon as he introduced himself: 'I have ten years' experience at the Centre, doing decontamination, so I know what I'm talking about. What I don't know is where to start, because I only have an hour to tell you everything. They've cut down my session, it used to last all afternoon!'

Or was it the subject of his talk, which could be summed up in one sentence as: how do we set about getting rid of the radioactivity a person has on or inside himself? It is a subject to which no one in the place is indifferent.

The session opened with a film that detailed and commented on the medical supervision that everyone working in a nuclear environment undergoes. The chief impression left by the film was that this industry is among the safest and best supervised so far as pollution is con-cerned. If an operator does accidentally receive some external irradi-ation or contamination, he is immediately scrubbed down and show-ered to get rid of anything noxious. Where the contamination is superficial, if necessary they perform what is known as 'exeresis', which involves ablation of the contaminated part. If toxic dust part-icles have been breathed in, the patient must inhale a drug in the form of a spray that traps radio-elements in the bronchial tubes. The same drug may also be painted on a wound or injected intravenously to prevent radioactive dust particles from settling in particular organs (liver, bones, lungs, or whatever).

After the film the nurse expanded a little on what had been said. Everyone who has been contaminated, once he has received the appropriate attention, undergoes spectrography – 'the coffin, right?' (actually a box in which the patient lies to be X-rayed) – and has his urine analysed over a twenty-four or forty-eight hour period (involv-ing the dreaded 'bottles'). As soon as these facts had been dispensed, the questions started flying:

The chap had his head washed – will there be any after-effects there?

Are the after-effects short-term or long-term?

What happens if you can't do shift work?

When is it not possible to wear a mask?

Where does it go, the water that's been used to scrub down people who've been contaminated?

Is anything known about the long-term risks resulting from contamination?

All these questions, showing open concern about the consequences of radioactivity or revealing a latent fear of being unfit to do the work required of one, generally received no precise answer. In any case, those who had asked them scarcely listened to the answers. They had simply wanted to talk, to give vent to their anxiety.

Faced with this flood of questions, the nurse resorted to humour:

There are fewer and fewer cases of contamination. At the Medical Department we might go for ten days without seeing one. It can get quite boring, in fact.

We wash their heads but we haven't ever shaved one.

You don't want to wear your best pair of pants to work because just occasionally something will occur . . . But we take good care of 'little Willie' [*le petit outil*], we don't want anything happening to him!

This latter observation was the only one containing any allusion to the potential effects of radioactivity on virility. The trainees never mentioned the subject, at least not openly, although it must be one that preoccupies them because the nurse felt obliged to give this spontaneous reassurance. Similarly, by stating in humorous terms that 'we haven't ever shaved one' he was offering an answer to the rumours suggesting that 'people who work at the plant are all bald, their hair falls out . . . ' and thus indirectly claiming that if you stay there you will lose your manhood.

At the end of the session I took the nurse aside and asked him whether he had ever noticed any anxiety among workers who had been involved in a contamination incident. 'No, that's not a problem. What they don't like is the business of the sample bottles, they don't want to tell the wife they've been contaminated, maybe she won't want anything to do with them after that! So I tell them to say we're checking their albumin level.'

Those few words were heavy with implications. One sensed that, notwithstanding all the attention they received, these men were afraid of becoming contagious. Present also, beneath the surface, was the old medieval ostracism that used to weigh on those whose jobs were seen as repellant and whom women would not touch, particularly if they bore obvious signs of their occupation on their person (such as dyers, for instance, with their blue hands and fingernails). In this nuclear universe, where everything is invisible, it is the urine bottles that have become the outward and visible signs of danger and beyond that of infamy.

Torn between anxiety about the possible consequences of 'copping a dose' and fear of rejection by their wives, workers may understandably prefer to say nothing about any incidents in which they may be involved.

To press home his advantage or at least avoid being knocked off-balance by the avalanche of questions and requests for confirmation, our nurse repeatedly chose to relativise the consequences of the particular kind of radioactivity encountered at the la Hague plant. Ordinary accidents were often more serious, he pointed out: 'Better ten persons contaminated than ten falling off a piece of scaffolding.' Or, even more to the point, the radioactivity a person is carrying does not always come from the plant but from elsewhere. 'Depend on it, at the "spectro" we find contamination that has nothing to do with the Centre but comes with the compliments of our friends in the East.'

The nurse was alluding here to the anomalies revealed by a number of spectrographs of plant personnel that were carried out a few months after the Chernobyl accident. Their print-outs showed unusual peaks in the caesium area, which the Medical Department attributed to contamination by fall-out from the cloud that passed over Europe after the disaster. Since then, these unusual images have been said to feature 'the ghost of Chernobyl'.

Whether the nurse was being ironical or relativising, everything he said exuded a sense of blame, as if becoming irradiated or contaminated was the price to be paid for working in this invisible world. That, it seemed to me, is how we should understand this unfortunate expression, uttered in a moment of inattention: 'At the Medical Department we wait for the victim . . . ' Or this answer given to a trainee who had asked about differences in medical treatment as between COGEMA and non-COGEMA staff: 'Everyone is treated in the same way' (for which read: everyone is entitled to the same medical care on the site) and the added comment: 'We all get the same punishment' (for which read: you'll get irradiated just the same).

And then there was this sentence, right at the end: 'You know, it's not as bad as AIDS, contamination . . . '

These words insinuating blame, this whole discourse with its incidental talk of culpability, must make an indelible impression on trainees!

6 The nuclear everyday

Imagine the state of mind in which most of the technicians taken on at the la Hague plant found themselves:

> I'm from Lorraine originally, started off in the iron and steel industry, but we soon realised that was on its last legs. Then in 1977 COGEMA put an ad in one of the eastern newspapers ... I've worked my way up. Getting in here was like getting into NASA, you were headed for the realms of high-tech.

> La Hague, COGEMA ... meant nothing at all to me to begin with, what I mainly thought was that working in nuclear energy was like working at the sharp end of industry ...

> I didn't know much about nuclear energy, but for me it represented the future ...

Things are different now. Young people entering the plant today know where they stand as regards the risks to which they will be exposed. Yet they all banish their anxiety with the same refrain: 'There's less risk in working here than there is in taking your car out each morning.'

That leaves them with the avowed satisfaction of having a steady job and pride at having access to the latest equipment: 'What's good here is that COGEMA has a huge budget and if there's any new machinery they buy it straight away. We're up at the forefront of technology. The engineers are always going on trips to look at and find out about new equipment.'

But ex-employees and new recruits agree in stating that high technology is no substitute for an interesting job. Some recall nostalgically: 'In the old days we did things because it was "our" plant, we were involved and we were also all mates, so we got organised to make a go of it.' Others acknowledge that; 'It's interesting to start with, working at the plant, afterwards it becomes a bore!' And they all say: 'When you've seen the way they work on-limits ... not specially effective, sometimes plain stupid ... It makes you think ... The very latest technology soon proves inadequate when it comes down to the reality of the job.' 'The work's 90 per cent routine with no say of your own.'

One source of tedium is the sheer size of the establishment: 'Before there were two rest rooms, now there are maybe fifteen . . . People are scattered about and no longer know one another.' Another source is the complexity of the reprocessing operation, which leads to a compartmentalisation of the various shops, laboratories, and other treatment stations. All these units are involved in the same process, but they take no notice of one another. Each one acts on its own account.

One young female lab technician complained of the lack of professional relations and exchange of ideas between shops:

> We do routine checks on the concentration of radioactive products in the water in the ponds. Occasionally, when the plant is having problems, we do special analyses of precipitates that form where they ought not to. That's more interesting, except we're not told anything about the operation, we have no idea where the stuff comes from, at what point it formed . . . And afterwards we don't know what they do with our findings!

In other words, the purpose of an experiment, the significance of a particular activity, may elude those charged with carrying it out.

Boredom further arises out of the repetitive nature of the jobs (chopping up uranium rods with the aid of remote handling gear, using a press to compact drums of waste one after another) or their monotony (watching control panels or computer screens). Moreover, these features are tending to become more marked as technology progresses. With the object of improving safety, the trend is towards more and more automation of production tasks and a greater and greater degree of computerisation of control functions. Man, regarded as the weak link in the man/machine partnership, is gradually being eliminated. In the new UP3 plant, all the technical solutions have been worked out with this in mind, giving rise to a fresh problem, namely the possible psychological consequences of this kind of marginalisation of man at work.

> Working in UP3 will be very different, the plant is almost entirely computer-controlled, which means the work will be of a more abstract nature. The operator will have screens in front of him, showing the network of rooms, and he will have to imagine what is actually going on in there, not just in two but also in three dimensions. It'll be a watching and waiting job, monotonous and sedentary, and he'll have to be able to put up with such working conditions, on top of which there will be essential safety instructions and physical checks. These are the job criteria by which we select technicians.

The speaker was the psychologist in charge of recruiting technical staff. His statement echoes those of trade unionists who are also concerned with these problems:

We're getting rather worried about the future of relations between man and machine . . . What the man does with his machine . . . Sitting in front of a television screen with centralised control, if he's not really familiar with his equipment he's not necessarily going to be able to follow what's going on or be properly aware of when an incident or an accident occurs. If a person is bored or feels he's over-qualified for the job he's being asked to do, there's a risk he'll lose his motivation, in which case he's not going to keep up with his equipment, he's not going to try and improve his tool, he's not going to be trying to do anything . . .

Lack of interest leads to a loss of vigilance, and the thing that makes this all the more serious and causes it to set in the more swiftly is this tendency to represent the machine or the tool as being wholly reliable, so much so, in fact, that those who design or use them will sometimes refuse to believe that their instruments might be faulty in any way.[1] The other side of this reliability on the part of the equipment is that the people who operate it are required to comply with a growing number of safety directives that add to the burden of the regulations to be observed and the repetitive nature of the checks that need to be carried out. 'It's more and more a matter of following orders and filling in forms. You spend the whole night filling notebooks, doing the rounds, doing your rules of three . . . That's what an operator's job is now. You don't need to be a technician to press buttons!'

Asking skilled technicians to perform such simple, relatively lowly tasks does not enable them to express the full range of their abilities or expertise. Too much safety is boring, and boredom spawns the *desire for risk*. 'You sometimes find yourself hoping for a problem, be it mechanical or chemical, even nuclear, involving contamination, even if that's not what you really want . . . You're watching for the snag, the little hiccup, you know . . . Because the job's an awful bore apart from incidents!'

On top of the monotony, the wearisome uniformity of movement, and the plethora of orders and checks to be carried out, there is the effect of a certain kind of language, namely the somewhat belittling language used by the training-course instructor and by others in positions of responsibility to describe the tasks involved in the reprocessing of spent nuclear fuel. Think of the words borrowed from the vocabulary of cooking and housekeeping that were used during the course. Described in such terms, the tasks that these men are required to perform in irradiated or contaminated areas appear to bathe in a world where everything is safe, imbued with an almost domestic bliss. They can bring little satisfaction, either real or symbolic. The *feminine* guise in which those tasks are represented, emphasising their benign if not innocuous aspect, renders virtually intolerable work that is in fact performed under extremely arduous physical conditions (in vinyl suits, amid heat and noise, at great speed) and carries incalculable biological consequences. These men are working in the most modern nuclear installation in the world, doing jobs that may be dull but are none the less dangerous, and people speak to them in the kind of language that is normally reserved for women.

In the circumstances, what satisfaction is to be gained from carrying out operations on-limits and fulfilling functions that, because of the danger involved, will always engender a certain amount of anxiety, even if it is denied and suppressed? What motivation is a man to find day after day to help him perform tasks that may be jeopardising his physical integrity?

To adapt to this system of constraints and controls, to push aside anxiety, triumph over fear, and render boredom tolerable, workers in the nuclear industry use certain tricks of language and exploit certain flights of fancy. Taking the language that is used to describe their jobs, these men proceed to make it their own. In doing so, however, they transform it. They subvert it by adding words, employing metaphors, and adopting peculiar turns of phrase to such effect that they contrive to shatter it from within and recover an image of themselves that is more rewarding than the one that takes such a beating from the hierarchy.

In place of the official scientific presentation of work in a nuclear environment they substitute their own language, their own interpretation, their own way of seeing it and 'having their being' within it. In short, they refashion an industrial world to suit themselves.

The kamikaze and the *rentier*

When talking about themselves, people who work in the French nuclear industry divide themselves into two categories. On the one hand there are the *rentiers* ('person living on dividends from property, investments, etc.' (*COD*), i.e., a byword for caution; Tr.), who before venturing 'on-limits' will make sure that every precaution has been taken, even going to the lengths of working out other types of precaution that they feel might be more reliable. On the other hand there are the *kamikazes*, men who are always prepared to work 'on-limits' without bothering too much about the safety regulations, men for whom speed and efficiency (getting the job done in the shortest possible time) will always take precedence over safety.

Both labels relate to the notion of risk: calculated risk in the case of the first group, risk courted in the case of the second. *Rentiers* invent procedures that they believe will enable them to manage their 'dose' capital in their best interests, which in this context means they try to keep their levels as low as possible. Kamikazes, on the other hand, approach radioactivity quite fearlessly (or perhaps unwittingly), regardless of any 'doses' they may accumulate. The *rentier* manages risk 'like a good family man'. The kamikaze approaches it in the manner of a 'warrior' who scorns danger but who may, of course, be going to his death . . . We all know the fate that awaited the kamikaze.

The people in charge of recruitment are well aware of these two types of behaviour, these two attitudes towards danger. Indeed, they seek to identify them among candidates in order to steer them towards the jobs best suited to their individual temperament and to the exigencies of production.

> Kamikazes are found mainly in the mechanical part of the plant because there you have to get stuck in. In the chemical part there's a different mentality, there you get mainly *rentiers*. Maybe it has something to do with the history of the plant and the fact that there were more militant trade-unionists in the chemical section who took a very firm line on safety. I don't know. But it's true, there are two ways of dealing with poor working conditions: either you demand more money in compensation, or you demand greater safety. On the mechanical side the operators will ask for an extra allowance. The chemists will plunge into months of talks before coming up with a programme for reorganising the workplace and providing rest periods. It's a case of two different ways of seeing things.

Be they kamikazes or *rentiers*, however, all nuclear workers agree in the way in which they talk about the risks they run, the doses they find themselves receiving, and the many perils they face when working 'on-limits'.

For instance, you will hear people who have 'copped a dose' exclaim:

> We got ourselves a fix.
>
> We got our balls loaded [*On a pris plein les couilles*].
>
> We got lit up.
>
> We took a bellyful.
>
> We were pumped full of lead.
>
> We got our whiskers stiffened [*On a pris plein les moustaches*].

Words that speak of maleness and sexuality, expressions redolent of virility, of potency, a vocabulary for men who look danger in the face. So many verbal attempts, in short, to counteract the rumours that circulate incessantly, alleging that workers in the nuclear industry are not 'real' men.

And when talking of radioactive matter, technicians will exclaim: 'That's farting like a good'un . . .' (*ça pète pas mal*) or 'It's spitting like hell . . .' – metaphors that evoke the clash of arms and the din of battle, turns of speech that transform the culinary language normally offered to them (with its 'soups' and 'juices' and 'gravies') into a war chant. Yet another way, in fact, of modulating feminine into masculine and taking a verbal stand against the encroachments of women upon a world made for men.

Actually, not all workers talk about radioactivity in this way, especially not women.

The engineers, as members of management, prefer to speak of *fifrelins*,[2] a term that carries a note of contempt, indicating how little importance they attach to any doses of radioactivity they may receive. The attitude of scornful indifference affected by certain engineers with regard to radioactive pollution is in fact notorious. As a member of the Radioprotection Department recalled:

> I saw an engineer who had become contaminated through visiting a building. He was in street clothes, an ordinary suit, you know, because they don't wear overalls, not those fellows! When they noticed at the exit control they tried to stop him . . But there was nothing they could do, they had to let him go. 'Do you realise who you're talking to?' he said, and off he went home in that state.

The higher up people are in the hierarchy, the less heed they pay to these 'trifles' that irradiate everything around them!

> The physicists, the research people, they're the worst of all! They think they're above the rules. You know those target-holders, little discs that have become irradiated, they wrap them in a newspaper, pop them in the briefcase, and it's off home to Paris . . . The doses aren't large, but it gives you some idea of the way they think!

I was told this by a radioprotection officer attached to one of the research laboratories.

As for the female technicians who work on-limits, they avoid putting a name to radioactivity. They will speak of 'something' or simply 'it', as in 'I said to myself, I've got something on me' or 'It spreads everywhere.'

Do they believe they are warding off the danger by refusing to name it, or are they, through the pronoun, alluding to the hidden, invisible aspect of radioactivity? Women (the ones I met, at least) manifest a very different attitude towards radioactivity than do men. They admit to being scared of it. They acknowledge their anxiety regarding its potential biological effects.

> I don't feel as easy in my mind working here as I would somewhere else. When an analysis arrives and I know it's radioactive, I try to stay calm, but it's easier said than done . . . And then every month when the film results come back and I find I've been contaminated, that really gets me! Especially if I've taken a bit more than I expected.

And they will confess anxiously: 'I always have the feeling I'm taking something home on me!'

'It' sticks to their skin! The skin being an organ that, for a woman, constitutes the membrane within which life is born and sustained. Hence their understandable anxiety in the face of this nuclear world inhabited by invisible powers. What is more, they know they are subject to a special regulation banning them from any ionising environment as soon as they exhibit the first signs of pregnancy. Is that sufficient? Might they not have unsuspected long-term effects, those impalpable, deadly emanations? It is a huge question and a never-ending torment, for no one can give them the answer. As wives and mothers, these female technicians are afraid of jeopardising their own power to give life. The fantasies that have always hovered around the phenomenon of gestation and that the march of scientific know-ledge was beginning to dispel have undoubtedly found fresh strength in this world haunted by invisible but intensely noxious waves. This makes it easier to understand certain admissions from women that seem to adumbrate a fear of giving birth to 'freaks'. Such fears and anxieties do in fact find more or less explicit expression among the women who live in the vicinity of the reprocessing plant and whose husbands and sons work there.

So what is at issue psychologically in one and the same reality will differ according to the sex, occupation, and social status of the subject. Women talk about radioactivity in allusive terms. Management engin-eers pretend nonchalance. Technicians translate it into male energy. However, these various semantic strategies are not, in themselves, sufficient to banish fear and refashion a world in which a person may live and work without too much anguish. To achieve that sort of mastery over the dangers incurred, other forms of conjuration are required, other ways of representing the industrial world.

Strength and decay

Listening to these people talk about the dangers of radioactivity, you very soon become aware that they draw a subtle distinction between irradiation and contamination. In their eyes, the two dangers are not of the same order. Irradiation, caused by the rays emitted by a nuclear substance, is seen in a positive light. Here images of 'cleanness' come high on the list; ideas of 'strength' and 'power' loom large. By contrast, the contamination that arises from contact with radioactive dust particles is thought of in negative terms and associ-ated with an impression of 'filth', allied to the notion of 'decay'.

'You cop doses, you get irradiated . . . It's true you may be putting your life at risk . . . But you're tough, for heaven's sake . . .' 'Contamination's not the same, it's disgusting . . . shitty . . . you're messed up [*daubé*[3]] . . . you're rotten.'

Simplifying somewhat, we get the following sequences:

IRRADIATION	CONTAMINATION
RAY	DUST
CLEAN	DIRTY
STRENGTH	DECAY
'you're tough'	'you're rotten'

Why should the apparently heterogeneous notions introduced into each sequence be grouped together in a single category? What properties do they have in common? What system of explanation underlies the coherence suggested by the words?

It is worth noting that each of these terms, irradiation and contamination, possesses a double meaning, a fact that will surely not have escaped those who use them on a daily basis. Both of them play on a literal sense and a figurative sense that carries obvious moral overtones. *Irradiation*, in everyday parlance, is 'an emission of light rays'.[4] In the figurative sense, the word takes on the idea of a benign influx of warmth or radiance. The French word *contamination* has since the fourteenth century had the meaning 'blemish resulting from some unclean contact',[5] in both the physical and moral senses of 'unclean'. Granted, the medical vocabulary from which use of the term in a nuclear setting is derived relates back to the Latin connotation of the word, which contains no more than the idea of 'communication by contact'.[6] However, it looks very much as if the French folk memory has retained only the former acceptance, which spread under the influence of the Catholic church.

Irradiation: a word that evokes bright light, bedazzlement, and invokes myths of the regeneration of man through light (the phoenix, for example, being reborn from its ashes in a great burst of flame). It is a word to which people may also, more prosaically, attach images drawn from those television programmes featuring a 'superman' who, having been subjected to the influence of nuclear radiation, exhibits prodigious strength in everything he does. It is a bit like the 'burn' you get from alcohol, the *eau-de-vie* that is supposed to give men strength, indeed life! More powerfully, more radically still, the films shown during training courses relate how in the dawn of our world it was radioactive radiation that enabled life to emerge. Men have never had much difficulty in finding reasons to glorify irradiation.

Contamination plays in a different register entirely. This term, with its connotations of 'blemish' and 'corruption', is invariably, in the nuclear context, associated with 'dust', a word that in turn relates to such concepts as 'filth' and 'rubbish' and, in our Christian societies, beyond that to death. 'You are dust, and to dust you shall return'.[7]

These nuclear dust particles, these invisible dejecta, taint and corrupt a person, making him 'rotten'. It is a rottenness, a decay that leads to biological and social disorders. The contaminated person is regarded as sick (and does indeed receive prompt and elaborate medical attention). Above all, he may spread the contagion around him, upsetting the whole social order.

Wives do in fact refuse to have sex with husbands who have been contaminated. Anne, twenty-three, married to a temporary deconta-minator, told journalists who came to interview her: 'When I saw him come home with his bottles I was scared to touch him. I had to control myself. It was daft because there was no risk to me ... but I was pregnant.'[8]

Insidiously, contamination comes between couples, breaching the social order. It is understandable, in the circumstances, that men should choose to say nothing, inventing other excuses to account for the shaming bottles. 'My husband says nothing about what goes on up there. He never tells me anything. Sometimes I see him come home with his hands all red and swollen as if they'd had a good scrubbing. Once or twice I asked what had happened. He told me: "It's nothing." So I don't ask any more.'

Around the contaminated man, nothing is said. It is a way of marginalising him, of holding him at a distance. No doubt these women have realised that their silence helps 'their' menfolk to bear this feeling of gradual decomposition, this burden of risk, but it is at the cost of something being repressed on both sides.

Contamination may occur through the medium of objects or tools that are perhaps not tainted in themselves but that simply by virtue of belonging to the world of *le nucléaire* have no place outside it. Otherwise there is a danger of their spreading confusion by effecting an overlap between what as a rule are mutually exclusive worlds. 'I hate him bringing anything from the plant back to the house!' exclaimed Isabelle, a thirty-five-year-old schoolteacher, when her husband, a technical operator, took from his pocket the film-badge that he had forgotten to leave in its proper place. In the village of Flamanville there was once a rumour that a woman had fallen ill after her husband, who worked at the nuclear power station, had installed central heating in his house with tubing 'borrowed' from work!

From sexual ostracism to defiling the family home, contamination leads to all kinds of social disturbance. Understandably, people try to steer clear of it.

Incidentally, the work of linguists and ethnologists has shown that 'order' and 'disorder' constitute the foundation of all social organisation. In his *Vocabulary of Indo-European Institutions*,[9] Emile Benveniste writes as follows:

> Order. This is one of the key notions of the legal as well as of the religious and moral worlds of Indo-Europeans: it is 'Order' that governs the disposition of the universe, the movements of the stars, and the periodicity of the seasons and the years as it governs the relations between men and gods and ultimately among men themselves. Nothing that has to do with man and the world escapes the dominion of 'Order'. It is thus the foundation, both religious and moral, of all society; without this principle, everything would revert to chaos.

Investigating the definition of what is 'dirty' in the eyes of primitive societies, Mary Douglas has shown that it is in fact a relative idea, part of a symbol system through which a culture organises the sensible world, with the result that 'thinking about dirt implies thinking about the relationship of order to disorder, being to non-being, form to formlessness, and life to death'.[10]

These remarks may be transferred to the nuclear domain. In this invisible, impalpable, inaudible world the human imagination does its usual job of restoring to that world the kind of materiality and humanity that will enable man to comprehend and move within it. Through the medium of symbolic thought, the perils of nuclear energy are slotted into what societies know and have always known.

The nuclear industry does not only furnish words for conceptualising its dangers; it also supplies technical properties on which a system of representations can be hung.

The training course, whether through the instructor, through the nurse, or through the films shown, dealt mainly with 'contamination'. 'Irradiation' was scarcely mentioned, probably because it is harder to detect with monitoring instruments. As one radioprotection expert explained to me:

> A person can become irradiated, go through all the controls, and leave the building without anything happening, without setting off a single alarm. Once you've left the source of irradiation, it stops. Actually, it goes on irradiating inside the fellow and the damage done by that irradiation remains, but it can't be measured because here all the measuring instruments at the exits of the buildings are for contamination. To find out if there are any particles left in the hair, on the hands ... But if you've just spent an hour in front of a source of irradiation that has destroyed a few cells, it doesn't show up on such monitoring devices. That will be detected during a medical inspection or when the film-badge results come back ... But it's very unusual for an immediate connection to be drawn between cause and effect ... A person is told: 'You're tired!' It happens, no one asks too many questions. From there to thinking that irradiation is something

you always get away with . . . well, it's not a big step! That's how people are able to say they're tough.

On the one hand, then, there is irradiation, which is not detected immediately, which can be concealed from oneself and others, and which a person may try to ignore or forget about, even though he knows that it goes on lurking, like some invisible yet voracious beast, deep inside him. On the other hand there is contamination, which triggers the alarms, alerting one and all to the fact that an incident has occurred. As a result, the eyes of the group are inevitably turned on the person who has caused the rumpus, and the general reaction is to give that person a wide berth. As witness what happened to this visitor to the plant when her watch set off the dreaded sound signal during the exit controls. In the coach back to town everyone kept well away from her, leaving her sitting on her own in a corner like someone with the plague!

Irradiation is seen as something superficial, fleeting, momentary. In talking about it, people will say casually: 'I copped a dose' or 'I got a dose.' With irradiation a person is still on the side of order. In this plant devoted to reprocessing waste (*déchets*), he symbolically escapes the world of filth (*ordure*).

Contamination, however, is experienced as penetrating flesh and blood. It may be inhaled or ingested, whence this definition that workers give of it: 'Contamination is when you've eaten a dose.' And men speak of it as 'shit' (*merde*), while women talk of 'poo' (*caca*). The contamination produced by the 'waste' reprocessed in this plant is regarded as particularly fearsome because it spreads through the medium of excremental dust particles. Decomposition then sets in, and the result is disorder.

Playing on these notions of clean and dirty, strength and decay, and order and disorder, workers at the plant have recreated a world of coherence, a world of their own on which they can then seek to get a purchase in order to prove their power and their ability to brave and surmount the perils of *le nucléaire*.

It is not a game that can be taken very far, because the players know full well that too much exposure to sources of irradiation or contamination will eventually lead to death. There is, however, a small area of freedom, a gap (perhaps the one left by managing the doses a person is 'permitted') in which it is possible to play with fire. The game (or rather, the tricks, the word 'game' (*jeu*, which also denotes 'gambling'; Tr.) being probably excessive in this context) may take two directions: either these men confront radioactivity directly, or they endeavour to make themselves masters of it by avoiding it. Both approaches in fact amount to the same thing, namely denying the danger that threatens. Both tactics have the same objective: being able to bear the burden of fear that is implicit in the job.

The magic of nuclear power

Men will employ these tactics in accordance with their temperament (whether kamikaze or *rentier*) but above all in accordance with the system of representations that they have worked out (order or disorder, strength or decay).

Kamikazes, as true soldiers of nuclear energy, prefer a clean, manly war fought in terms of direct confrontations with irradiation, a danger that threatens particularly in the mechanical section of the plant, where not surprisingly a large number of kamikaze technicians are to be found. To wage his war, the kamikaze will employ various tactics. He may, for instance, exceed orders as regards exposure times. Alternatively, he may (deliberately or unwittingly) neglect to take all the usual precautions before embarking on a job. Examples are the operators who will actually manhandle the drums filled with radioactive waste or the ones who work in the shearing shop and by-pass the elaborate safety measures that slow down the rhythm of production.

> You find the kamikazes in the shops where things don't always go according to plan. At the top of the plant the spent fuel comes in, is removed from its packing, and is then cut up and dissolved ... But the spent-fuel containers have to be emptied out ... and that's not funny. The stuff gets jammed and needs to be unblocked. I've known crackpots who have gone in with a crowbar to unjam stuff in what we call a duck's beak, that's a sort of pipe with a bend in it. Afterwards it's not difficult to shunt this or by-pass that,[11] but these are safety factors we're taking about! Shifts may not pass on the orders, people forget, but it's gambling with safety. Each shift gets by as best it can, but hiccups can occur ...

It is mainly among the kamikazes that, under the influence of words, radioactivity becomes transformed into male energy, into sexual potency. 'In the engineering shops people take risks to prove that they're men ... It's a way of saying, "I'm not scared"!'

For them the irradiation incident becomes something to talk about, breaking the monotony of the job: 'I wonder if they aren't quite happy to have copped a little dose ... Now they have a story to tell ... At last, something happened to them one day ... They can talk about it ...' The comment was made by an operator with reference to two technicians who had suffered slight irradiation while repairing pipework in an '800' zone. He added: 'And after all, they'd got a dose, they hadn't caught AIDS ... I think a person's more annoyed about becoming contaminated than about copping a dose.'

Here again we have the contamination-blemish idea as something a person must seek to guard against or keep under control. Since contamination is particularly to be feared in the chemical part of the establishment, that was predictably where the greatest concentration of *rentier* technicians was to be found. Such people are all the more cautious about managing their 'dose capital' for the fact that they are dealing with contamination. Control, for them, consists firstly in ensuring that this danger does not arise and secondly in seeking to understand any incident that does occur so as to evolve certain knacks, certain ways of doing things, 'tricks of the trade' that the old hands then try to pass on to the younger generation.

> When there's a puncture in a sleeve or a glove box, the person shields it with his body, calls his mates to come and help, maybe one of them will then slip a face-mask on the one in a bad position and another bring a sleeve, ask him to move out of the way very carefully, and quickly slip the sleeve on ... With two old hands it works a treat. Whereas the normal tendency when a sleeve gives is to panic ... You've had it when that happens ... it means months of decontamination, you must wear a mask to work in the place for months before it's all cleaned up. Basically, the key to protection is ventilation and the way you take your hand out. When there's a break in the seal, the draught has to be going in the same direction, so if you make a sudden movement you risk stopping the draught and catching it yourself. That's something you have to know ... It's no good saying you only have to wear gloves and everything'll be all right.

To control contamination more effectively a person may in fact choose to confront it with his bare hands.

> I personally work without gloves, because with gloves you take them off and you don't check yourself. If a glove's punctured you don't notice. Whereas working bare-handed you check yourself more often. If you come out of a glove box you don't automatically think of checking yourself, but bare-handed it's a different matter! That way you don't spread contamination all over the place ...

These tricks and tactics, by giving a man the feeling that he can get the better of adversity (in this case contamination or irradiation), introduce little cracks into the monolithic complex of rules, orders, and obligatory systems by which he is usually bound. In an environment dominated by danger, man has contrived a chink of freedom. Through rediscovering the pleasure of playing a game, making up his own rules, working out his 'ploys', he turns the situation round, controlling the risk rather than being in perpetual thrall to it. These tiny, everyday procedures constitute so many defensive strategies to combat anxiety.

But there is more than just the pleasure of mastering a technological mechanism. With this concept of the 'knack', the nuclear worker has found a way of avoiding blame. Play is known to have a disjunctive role. In play it is 'every man for himself', or at least a person has his special partners – in this case, the shift he works with. But if they forget to inform the next shift, if they omit (which can happen, because in any game the 'ploys' remain secret) to explain what they have done to get round a particular safety measure, an incident may subsequently occur as a result of the ignorance in which the relieving shift has been kept. That shift may then quite rightly place the blame for the incident on the previous shift. 'Incidents are invariably caused by people not obeying orders.'

And if a worker, be he kamikaze or *rentier*, should chance to fall victim to an incident involving radioactivity, those who do not themselves subscribe to the belligerent kamikaze approach or to the wiles of the *rentiers*, as the case may be, are able to think: 'He had it coming to him.' Once again there is a human occasion at the origin of the mishap. Above all, it becomes easy to believe that if you make your own behaviour conform to the regulations you may escape the dangers that threaten you:

> In the nuclear industry there is a risk, but you have every means of protecting yourself, everything you need to deal with it, to keep a check on yourself. Plus the Radioprotection Department is there to keep an eye on things, to monitor whether or not you've received any doses. So in the normal course of events you're not in any danger!

One can see the symbolic effectiveness of these defensive strategies that locate the opening of hostilities elsewhere, off-loading the responsibility onto someone else, even if in the event the victim is self-confessedly consenting or even innocent. The important thing is that the original error can be pinned on a person, thus exculpating the technology on which the worker's safety depends. Given this kind of explanation, a person feels reassured. He knows what methods to employ in order to steer clear of danger, and if an incident occurs none the less, it is easy for him to say he is not to blame.

The only way to limit the risk of these dangerous 'games' is to tighten up the orders, create automatic responses, eliminate all desire for initiative.

> In theory you're not supposed to think about the orders. For instance, in the plutonium shop there are orders about critical mass. No one's ever going to disregard those because the stakes are too high, even if they know they're well below the norms and the risk is only potential. There no one is going to disobey orders, at least I should hope not. Otherwise the orders consist in following procedures. When there's a problem, if it's during the day you go up the hierarchy, if it's at night the duty supervisor deals with it

himself, either falling back on discipline or now he calls in a duty engineer who looks after coordination in the plant. There's very little initiative. Or what there is is minimal. Problems are caused by people taking the initiative in some way, hence the difficulty of keeping in full touch with what has been done before you, that's an enormous potential risk . . . That's the danger, people are bound together . . . There's a half-hour changeover period between shifts, each person at his work station briefs the one who's going to take his place.

Rules and regulations exert a stranglehold on the worker. So let it not be thought that these language games in which the technicians indulge, the system of representations with which they view the world of nuclear energy, have anything to do with fecklessness or immaturity. This is a deliberate mode of behaviour, an indispensable way of helping to render psychologically tolerable the boredom, the monotony, and (it would appear) the burden of anxiety arising out of their daily activities.

Without this way of thinking, without these organising exercises, and without these responses of denial or defiance, it would be impossible for them to go on working in such perilous realms, where man is in some sense an intruder. In failing to acknowledge this and ignoring the complexity of the man/workplace/technology equation, the nuclear-technology experts are in turn at risk of finding themselves facing some unexpected situations.

Apparently tamed or circumvented in this way, the dangers of nuclear energy become malleable, manageable. A person may then play with that energy in a positive way and on his own account, as we have just seen, like a sort of white magic that will ward off the perils surrounding him. He may, however, use it in the form of black magic, which is what happened in 1978 when a shiftworker, wanting to 'get back' at a foreman with whom he was not seeing eye to eye, placed some discs of irradiated metal under the seat of the man's car.[12] Radioactivity may, if the need arises, be harnessed in the service of revenge.

The medallions of the nuclear industry

Understandably, this idea of bracing oneself for danger and the daily employment of this virile, bellicose vocabulary can lead some people to wish to undergo a kind of nuclear 'baptism of fire' and hence unconsciously to provoke an incident (the 'snag' (*le pépin*) they all talk about, playing things down as usual). Indeed, it seems that until a person has received 'a dose', 'his dose', not only does he not have a story to tell; he remains in a condition of suspense, waiting for the incident that, statistically, is bound to occur. So it is plausible to see these provocative schemes as processes aimed at freeing the person who initiates them from an intolerable wait. Indeed, until a person has been the victim of an incident it is just as if he had not yet received his initiation and triumphed over the traumatism that that initiation brings, as it were changing the individual psychologically and bio-logically, causing him to advance from the state of novice to that of initiate, from man to superman.

This initiatory process is made all the more striking by the fact that each occasion when a person goes 'on-limits', each *passage* from one place to another, is accompanied by a series of rituals that act as so many processes of transformation. 'You have dressing and undress-ing every day. You change completely. There's a stage you go through, a sort of threshold you cross at the point where you change colour . . . I'm not saying your personality changes . . . But almost!'

A man is daily made ready to accomplish his initiation. Dressing, the time spent 'on-limits', and undressing constitute so many rituals of integration, aggregation, and then separation, marking the passage from one world to the other. Each day, whether a man doggedly avoids being soiled by contamination or deliberately brushes with manly irradiation, he duly performs the rites indispensable to his purification. The outfits that he dons and then throws away are the tangible objects of the proper unfolding of the rite. That gives them a special status: those vinyl membranes become true protective skins.

> In my laboratory I insist on no one using gloves to work. If they mess up their hands, too bad . . . But if they're wearing gloves that can't happen . . . They feel protected, don't even check themselves any more, and spread contamination everywhere, on the keyboards, on the telephone, without realising . . . You get secondary contamination all over the place!

However, it is impossible to say in advance how serious the incident will be and consequently how severe the traumatism. In this dangerous environment, where man is attempting to play tricks with the invisible, chance plays a not inconsiderable role. It would appear advisable, therefore, to kit oneself out with a few extra protections in order more effectively to keep it at bay. But where, in an industry that forbids the wearing of any personal objects and thus rules out recourse to the traditional fetishes of our Christian societies, are such things to be found?

I mentioned the way in which the training-course instructor pre-sented the organisation of worker-protection in an ionising environ-ment, how everything was said and demonstrated (with film back-up) in such a way as to persuade trainees that, so long as an operator follows the safety directives to the letter, no incident can occur. In other words, if you stick to the radioprotection technicians' instructions, if you dress properly, and if you are careful to carry the instruments that will measure the ambient radioactivity, you will be fully protected. No one will receive more than his permitted dose, as allotted to him in line with the official norms. Nothing is ever said (during the training course, at least) about the incidents that may occur (a punctured glove, a torn garment, a leaking pipe, a spillage) or about the elaborate procedures that are so essential if large-scale contamination or irradiation is to be avoided.

The training cycle does not include instruction in the 'tricks of the trade', the knacks acquired by old hands. A person may gain access to that sort of knowledge later, on the job, when doing shift work. In the absence of any direct transfer of such information, which might have provided trainees with skills enabling them to face danger and get on top of it without experiencing too much anxiety, a substitution occurs in the way in which the various measuring instruments are perceived. What happens is that they become actual means of protection. In other words, people no longer see these objects with which they equip themselves when going 'on-limits' for what they are, namely tools to measure ambient radioactivity; they see them as objects capable of affording protection.

Some technicians who had been working at the plant for more than ten years and were taking the course on a refresher basis voiced the same thought:

> The way in which worker safety is approached on the course is dramatic. You get the impression that the dosemeters and work suits are not just means of control and measurement but means of protection in their own right. If I'm wearing my dosemeter I'm protected ... Which is totally absurd ... A dosemeter isn't a charm for warding off bad luck!

A perfect illustration of this in concrete terms was contained in the laconic reply given by one technician when I asked him whether he experienced any apprehension at going on-limits: 'None at all ... Anyway, I'm protected, I have a chest film badge, a wrist film badge, even a pen-dosemeter.'

No need here of crosses or of effigies of the Virgin or one's patron saint. No need to commend oneself to God or his saints before starting on a job. The firm supplies its own protective medallions.

The symbolic transformation undergone by these objects explains or at least renders comprehensible certain modes of behaviour that I was told about but never managed to observe or verify (it was always 'other people' who acted in this way, never the speaker). I was told, for instance, that there was a 'traffic in films' on the site! Unexposed film badges were stolen from the shops and replaced by used ones. Why? Presumably, for these 'medallions' to be effective they must be without blemish. Hence these substitutions in which some people allegedly indulge. How is one to know? Whom is one to believe?

Guilt and punishment

You do not play with fire or try to outsmart radioactivity with impunity. Sooner or later you will have to pay. Had not the nurse stated on the training course: 'We all get the same punishment'?

Everything to do with the manipulation of the atom, whether it be releasing its energy for conversion into electricity or, as at la Hague, recycling nuclear substances, is unconsciously experienced in the public mind as a transgression ineluctably inviting chastisement. And the first to be punished, of course, are those who come closest to radioactive matter, namely the men and women who work in the nuclear industry.

Their punishment may take many forms. It may affect them directly, or it may strike at their families. It may manifest itself immediately or at a later date, long after they have ceased to work at the plant. For some the punishment may never come. For others it lies in the future. For one or two it is there already, taking the form of cancer, an illness that is often seen in terms of punishment undermining a person's physical integrity.

If people are able to speak of punishment in connection with cancer, it is because, for the sufferer, the disease is accompanied by a feeling of blame, as evinced by the fact that they will conceal it from themselves or refuse to talk about it. 'I know one man who died of leukemia. He wouldn't say anything, didn't even want to talk about it in case it was classified as an occupational disease. It's like that with lots of people. When they have cancer they don't want to talk about it!'

Sick people will generally refuse to sign the papers that would get them recognised as suffering from an occupational disease. Granted, the administrative procedures tend to be lengthy and meticulous and the legislation concerning occupational disease not easy for workers to exploit.

> It's up to the attending physician to make a declaration of presumption of occupational disease, which leads to an inquiry and a whole process of very complicated investigations ... So the initial step is never taken, the local doctors don't even mention the possibility to their patients ... We've tried, as a trade-union, to get doctors into good habits, but we've not succeeded ... Ever. So people don't say anything. You can also wait until the fellow's dead and go and see his widow, but you need an expert opinion, the body has to be exhumed ... You get the picture, it never works ... Not surprising, really. So there's no note on the file. It doesn't

find its way into COGEMA's epidemiological statistics. Whenever you try to do a study of cancer at the plant, it never works.

The silence that tends to surround this particular illness at every level confirms those afflicted by it in their feeling of culpability. Why is it never mentioned anywhere?

Yet a person need not be directly affected in physical terms for the idea of guilt to crop up, the notion of a price to be paid. You only have to listen to these men and women talking about the biological misfortune that will inevitably befall them one day. There are those, for instance, who believe that illness will eventually strike them down, and at the least physiological irregularity uncovered during their twice-yearly examinations they will panic and start to question the veracity of the diagnoses proposed by the establishment's Medical Department. 'I don't believe that "ghost of Chernobyl" story! They gloss over any abnormality in the blood formula by saying "it's because of Chernobyl", but what's to say it's true? Chernobyl suits them fine! They're doing it to cover up the illness . . .'

The wives are no less suspicious. One whose husband left the plant some years ago admitted: 'It haunts me even now! Because he did get contaminated . . . He took some big doses . . . and cancers can take twenty years to show . . . So it's still on my mind!' Another said anxiously:

Deep down I ask myself: 'Can you be sure? Aren't the analyses rigged? Isn't there always a tendency to play things down? I know perfectly well that the analyses aren't rigged, but can one ever be certain . . .?' And then it's all done according to norms. But a norm can be set anywhere, at any level. Are they reliable, those norms? Your norm won't be the same as mine. Oh, I don't talk to him about it, what's the use? I talk to him about his cigarettes instead . . . he smokes like a chimney, and that worries me more than his job. It's more concrete, too, more immediate, you can put your finger on it . . .

Smoking undoubtedly channels many fears relating to cancer. But because it is 'concrete', because 'you can put your finger on it', in this case it is probably also acting as the symbolic medium of a more muted and in any case incommunicable distress arising out of fear of *le nucléaire*.

Other workers seek to fend off this fear by making themselves less vulnerable, though they realise there is no escaping one's destiny:

I've had mates who've had cancer. One had cancer of the oesophagus, but he used to smoke two or three packets of cigarettes a day, another one drank and smoked – letting off both barrels, if you like! So is it a question of dose? Yes, there are cases of cancer up there, but you try to account for them by excesses of that sort . . . I don't smoke myself, and I don't drink . . .

Above all there is a swirl of expiatory rumour that surrounds those who work at the plant and that delivers its verdict whenever misfortune strikes a person's family. If a child is born with a deformity of some kind, even a hare-lip, or if a woman miscarries or suffers any prolonged illness, immediately word goes round: 'What do you expect – he works at the plant!'

Other rumours whisper that these men will be punished 'unto their children's children'. The saying goes that by working in the nuclear industry men lose their virility. They go bald. They cannot have children, or they have only daughters. It is even alleged that there was a fashion at the plant a few years ago for vasectomy. Was it for fear of engendering freaks? Rumour does not say. It is in the nature of rumour, of course, to speak in truncated images. You have to 'take my word for it'. An anonymous word that quotes no sources and names no names.

An ancestry discovered

To sustain this feeling of guilt, shatter this solitude, and adjust more easily to the rigours of anxiety, the men of la Hague have fashioned a collective memory, forged a certain self-awareness, and put together a destiny for themselves by latching on to an illustrious line of forebears: the miners.

Every account of work at the plant and of the risks incurred there is accompanied by a refrain on the subject of the miners of old: 'Our fathers went down the mine ... We work in the nuclear industry. They sacrificed their lives ... We put our lives at risk too.'

It is as if, by situating themselves in relation to a past where there was danger, they are reducing the very modern, very special sort of danger they face every day. 'Did silicosis ever stop miners' sons from going down the mine? Yet they knew what they were in for!'

The fact of having hit upon this line of descent (for that is indeed what they are claiming), of having forged this link with valiant ancestors, helps the nuclear worker of today to resign himself to a fate that has always existed, a destiny that none can escape. Since time immemorial men have laid down their lives that others might live in greater comfort. Workers in the nuclear industry are perpetuating the line of the great heroes of the modern age.

Conclusion
The ultimate subject: man

It may seem strange to end a book on the nuclear industry without taking up a position either for or against the exploitation of this form of energy. That, however, has not been my purpose.

I have tried in the foregoing chapters to capture something of the way in which the men and women who live alongside or work in such high-risk establishments relate to the phenomenon of radio-activity, the dangerous effects of which can neither be seen, nor felt, nor heard, and which they are led, purely through the medium of words or by resorting either to silence or to flights of fancy, to situate within such grids of interpretation as they have at their disposal.

The topic is a vast one, and I have certainly not said all that there is to be said on it. Indeed, I have chosen to trace a particular course, namely to focus attention on the turns of speech (and of silence), the procedures and strategems, the tactics and practices – in short – the whole spectrum of methods by which the people of la Hague deal with *le nucléaire*.

In so doing I have broken with an entire school of socio-anthropological research, particularly in the United States,[1] that has in essence set itself the task of measuring the influence of social structures on the perception of the many technological risks so characteristic of our modern societies with a view to finding improved ways of controlling and regulating them. Such studies demonstrate that risk is a complex, multi-faceted notion, a boundary object in fact, principally technical but also social and psychological, and one that is also the focus of much political and economic interest. They go on to postulate that, depending on the culture, social group, or historical period in question, risk has a variety of meanings and degrees of importance.

The next step in investigations of this kind is to try to understand the logic that appears to organise opinion regarding the danger incurred and to show that there are no general, abstract criteria of assessment governing calculations of risks by individuals, groups, or institutions. Douglas and Wildavsky,[2] for example, suggest that in Western societies individuals belong to groups organised in net-works. The nature of the boundaries defining groups and the scope for manoeuvre available to members situated within the networks serve to distinguish three types of society.

The first, typified above all by the engineer or the entrepreneur, even the scientist (men who are in some sense thrown upon their own resources), shows a propensity to seek out risk and accept the consequences. The second type takes in the administrator, the bureaucrat, all the people whose scope for freedom is restricted. They have their place in a powerful hierarchy and are therefore little inclined to take risks, seeking instead to guard against doing so by adopting a plethora of paralysing controls. The third type, finally, is embodied in the environmentalist, who, in order to gather into a tight network militants whose recruitment rate fluctuates, has a tendency to condemn wholesale all risks that threaten to destroy the planet. This categorisation does not cover all possible positions. What it does do is put forward 'the irreducible fact that within a single society of complex exchanges people are quite simply incapable of perceiving dangers in the same fashion because their local or specialised background moulds them into genuinely different beings'.[3]

The American approach could be described as both culturalist (each social group invents its own risk) and functionalist in that it seeks to understand the way in which risk (or disaster, when it occurs) ruptures the social fabric, shatters solidarities, and breaks up the human community. In other words, it is concerned with how societies experience the crisis situations induced by this 'risk civilisation'[4] that is ours today.

Such questions, interesting though they are, were not what attracted my attention. Admittedly, no major disaster has occurred at la Hague as yet. Nevertheless, what struck me as remarkable and indeed as crying out for an explanation was the fact that people there refuse to believe in the reality of this colossal technological risk. There was a need, it seemed to me, to try to define the mental processes, subtleties of language, or verbal strategies that enable both locals and plant workers to talk about nuclear disasters and at the same time deny that they could 'ever happen here'. In this sense Chernobyl furnished a language in which to discuss and a space in which to situate disaster *as such*. Such processes have ineluctable logical repercussions. They strengthen the technocrats' belief in the omnipotence of their technology, since they are able to state without fear of contradiction that 'the population at large is confident and reassured'.[5] As for the politicians, they find support for their position of having ceased to call for any kind of preventive review of the safety of local populations. For no emergency exercise has ever been undertaken at la Hague, and the special plan of action that was distributed to the inhabitants almost a quarter of a century ago has never been revised. The young teachers at the school in Beaumont, which lies within the sensitive area, deplored the fact that they had never received any emergency instructions whatsoever: 'If anything does happen we shan't know what to do!'

Is it fear of words that so paralyses people? It is just as if one ought never to mention the danger that threatens, never pronounce certain terms that speak plainly on the subject of risk and how to guard against it. At la Hague, *le nucléaire* exudes forgetfulness. It quite literally has the effect of creating memory blanks.

The studies I referred to earlier do not help to explain these instances of amnesia or elucidate these silences. They seek in the main to outline a kind of social morphology of the object 'risk', yet this is taken at such a level of generality that the end result is a real dilution of the notion. It becomes so vague as to lead one to question whether it really exists, since no one can agree as to its content. Between the catastrophism of the environmentalists, the immobilism of the bureaucrats, and the reassuring triumphalism of the technocrats, whom is one to believe? Whom is one to listen to?

But let us leave these controversies on one side for the moment. Granted, there are differences in the perception of danger according to the socio-cultural provenance of the individual concerned. What I wanted above all to show was that the sense of risk and the fear of danger exist in everyone, regardless of gender, social and occupational background, or professed opinion. Rumours and silences, conversational slips and diversionary tactics, subversion of words and objects, strategies of language, and processes of symbolisation constitute glaring evidence of the ordinary, everyday, familiar fear that stalks this place, permeating the lives of all who live in it.

This game of life and death is one that the men of the nuclear industry rehearse daily in their words and in their actions. Why has no one ever asked questions about the crazy risks they take when driving to and from work? And what of the nicknames they have rather touchingly, with more than a dash of black humour, bestowed on certain key features of the site? Are they altogether innocent? At the Medical Spectography Department, the box in which the patient is placed to measure the gamma radiation he has received is invariably referred to as the 'coffin'. The revolving gate that serves as one of the muster stations is 'the mincer'. The huge mound of earth that rises at the western end of the site and can be seen from everywhere is known to one and all as the 'molehill' ('rabbit warren' is the equivalent English figure of speech; Tr.), with its connotations of burial, and to some as 'the tomb of the cancer victims', which is scarcely more cheerful. The whole site is rather like a huge board game on which the workers have set out the various dangers that threaten them.

Plant employees enter and leave this obstacle-rich world by 'atom boulevard'. That is what they call the main road linking Cherbourg and the reprocessing plant, which at the time when I did my study had recently been widened. 'To make it easier to evacuate people . . . *They* expect an accident, you see', the inhabitants of the neighbouring hamlets mutter behind their hands.

All right, it could be said that this muted fear, which is more or less repressed but which is not difficult to detect when you are talking to the people of la Hague, is just something left over, a sort of clinker – no more significant than that. Given the irresistible movement of our societies towards what is called technical progress, involving the use of sophisticated technologies, we are obliged to disregard it. It is a remnant, a residue, so firmly under control, so shrunken, and now so insignificantly small that we tend to take no notice of it. I do not pretend to have an answer to the question of the dread suffered by modern societies. Nor do I have a solution to the contradictions thrown up by industrial progress in the context of the evolution of the world. I have simply tried to reveal, in terms of people's everyday experience (a subject that is too often overlooked), a hidden suffering on a modest yet real scale, indicating the stubborn persistence of a sickness in our civilisation.

Imagination will out

I detected this furtive anxiety not only among the people of la Hague but also among the technicians at the plant, if only in their ways of utilising the system of safety regulations, of dodging the issue as between irradiation and contamination, of playing tricks with words in order to recreate a world in which they can live and move and still retain a certain amount of freedom. Given this space where all is mechanisation and automation, men surreptitiously reintroduce tactics, practices, and a language borrowed from elsewhere. They find a thousand and one ways of, so to speak, prevaricating with an order that has been imposed on them from outside, the object being to make the anxiety that is bound up with this type of work more bearable, to place their own stamp on technical procedures that have been devised without consulting those concerned.

In this technological universe, man has given his imagination free rein. If this imaginary dimension of everyday life was taken into consideration, if these modes of behaviour dedicated to subverting the dominion of technology were used as a basis, and if some attempt was made to understand the ways in which men play about with machinery or with rules, a fresh approach might perhaps be envisaged that no longer sidelined the technician and effectively ignored him. It ought no longer to be possible to exclude the world of the imagination from any consistent approach to tackling the problems posed by work in our societies.

Some will see in these imaginative practices that have the effect of organising curious types of discourse a form of resistance to the upheavals of the modern era that currently has man in its grip. I do not believe that is true at all. With these turns of speech and these ways of doing things, people are not combating nuclear energy or rebelling against its use. Quite the opposite, in fact: all their various stratagems are so many tricks and tactics for taming the dangerous, unknown world in which these men and women not only have to live but need to go on living.

To assimilate this novelty, people borrow, albeit unwittingly, from the collective memory of the group. They draw on what, if you like, their society has *always known*, on the enduring facts and cultural messages buried in the social practices that get handed down from generation to generation. In a way, they are drawing on what in anthropology is often defined by the term 'tradition'.[6] It is traditional for Hagars to take a long-term view of the changes affecting their social and territorial environment. For example, the fact that the plant was built on land they regarded as foreign to them meant that it had its appointed place there. That made it easy for people to accept it, integrate it, even forget about it. A similar mechanism operated in the case of the evacuation plan, which, in providing for the peninsula to be cut off, coincided with the foundation myth of this society, whose destiny it is to become an island. Why, in the circumstances, fight against an establishment that since time immemorial had been meant to be there? These same processes of assimilation are now at work among plant personnel. Using the popular representations of contamination and irradiation, picking up the sense of rites of passage, and playing with words, they have contrived to fit this new thing, namely radioactivity, into the grids of a common wisdom. That done, it can be lived with, faced up to, even gambled with.

I do not propose to tackle the problem (which is far from having been resolved) of understanding these processes. Very little is known about how the collective memory takes shape and is handed down. The important thing to notice here is this welling up into the present of elements from the past, this irruption of a traditional imagination into a world in thrall to modernity. If we define modernity as the distinguishing characteristic of technological societies avid for change and innovation and prone to ceaseless self-questioning, it looks in the light of this Hagar experience as if one of the questions we should be asking ourselves very concretely is how well-founded such a definition is. Modernity has not swept tradition away. The fact is, tradition has a surprising way of re-emerging where we least expect it.

It is also a fact that nuclear energy has always, from the very earliest days, unleashed people's imaginations. The opinions advanced for or against its development are rarely based on technical or economic arguments alone. There is always a symbolic dimension to invest them with passion. When in the 1970s the French government took its decision to go 'all out' for nuclear power, discussion raged. The defenders of nuclear power played the 'prestige and necessity' cards.[7] Nuclear power, they said, was man's greatest conquest. It represented a genuine challenge to nature, flouting all her prohibitions. They elevated this area of technology almost to the level of the sacred. Moreover, the terminology, both scientific and journalistic, that came to be applied to nuclear power operated on the frontiers between sacred and profane, between inert and animate, and between human and non-human. For example, nuclear power stations became 'the cathedrals of the twentieth century'. They had a 'heart' (*coeur*; English refers to it as a 'core') that 'spread' (the French verb *diverger* means in this context 'to start a chain reaction'), and occasionally the tanks surrounding the reactors wept all the 'tears of nuclear power'.[8] As for the names bestowed on the products of this technology, they all bear the stamp of potency, of a gauntlet thrown down before nature. The French fast-breeder reactor is called *Super Phénix*. France's nuclear-powered submarines have names like *Le Redoutable*, *Le Terrible*, *Le Foudroyant* (*foudre* = lightning), *L'Inflexible*, and *Le Tonnant* (*tonner* = to thunder).

Given this type of Promethean affirmation, this clamour for an overstepping of bounds (remember that the name of the test site selected for the American bomb was adopted for that transgressive garment, the bikini), it was predictable that an equally impassioned opposition would rise up to inveigh against the desecrators of nature and oppose the overthrow of social values.

'Filth everlasting'[9]

It could be that nuclear power stimulates people's imaginations in this way because once its virulence has been unleashed there appears to be no way of ever appeasing it.

Every social group produces residues of some kind, rubbish that fits into the normal cycle of degeneration and rebirth characterising the living world. At the same time, however, in the popular mind this so-called 'natural' refuse is regarded with a certain amount of anxiety and mistrust. So much so, in fact, that it becomes marked with the seal of blemish and is seen as posing a threat to the social order. As for mythical thought, it connotes excrementa with appalling uproar and filth with an unbearable howling,[10] linkages that are generally accepted as expressing situations beyond civilised control.

Nowadays these themes, which one might expect to have been superceded by scientific thought, have been revived by the effects of the industrialisation of modern societies, the waste from which threatens the very survival of the planet.[11] With the nuclear industry, the question of how to get rid of used materials becomes particularly acute. There is no end to the production cycle of radioactive waste (not even reprocessing can eliminate it, since reprocessing incessantly creates fresh waste), just as there is no end to the time for which it must continue to be monitored, once stockpiled. The less active kinds need monitoring for some three hundred years, the more vigorous kinds for ever.

These dizzying time-scales have understandably overwhelmed those workings of the collective memory that still today weave human time. In this circular, stable time, past, present, and future are intimately bound up with and constantly interact with one another. 'Before', 'now', and 'tomorrow' are periodically wiped out by the perpetual recommencement of a sameness in which events are annulled and the ups and downs of History flattened out. For la Hague, that kind of time no longer runs. 'Now,' people say, 'nothing will ever get back to the way it was. The climate has changed, the weather's colder, it rains the whole time.' Neither nature, nor human knowledge, nor the memory of man can any longer measure themselves against the massive time-scale imposed by an industry that is burying beneath the floor of the plant, in the ancestral territory of the people of la Hague, drums of waste of which the radioactivity of certain elements will take perhaps 24,000 years to lose half its intensity.[12] These over-abrupt changes, together with this immeasurable chronology and ever-present risk, mean that here, in this place, the cycle can no longer engage. La Hague has made the transition, definitively, from cyclical time to linear time.

Is History (the kind made by man) in fact capable of assuming responsibility for the uninterrupted functioning of these noxious discharges and for ensuring the safety of these nuclear storage sites for millennia to come? Be it cyclical or linear, there is a big risk of time, at la Hague, getting out of man's control.

With nuclear power, the human race is caught in the trap of a new kind of dialectic. Man is not in this instance the master of every part of the productive process because the material on which he is working imposes a technical constraint (namely radioactivity) so great as to bind him with its own law. This fact alters man's perception of time, but it also changes his psycho-sociological relationships with matter –

that is to say, with nature. In nature, man's relationship to waste is fundamental, being bound up with filth or with uproar, both of which denote disorder and lead to death.

In the nuclear industry, however, waste, that last refuge of radio-activity, is omnipresent at three levels.

Technically: in the cycle of nuclear energy the elimination of spent fuel is the sector over which the engineers have least control. The societies of the West are today focusing anxiously on this problem, which so long as it remains unresolved encumbers the whole future development of the industry.

Sociologically: the stockpiling centres, which for the management of what is merely waste require highly sophisticated technical equipment, scare people. Consequently, the popular opposition that was once in evidence against the building of nuclear power stations is now directed against the construction of these storage sites.

And last, symbolically: with nuclear power man, like the sorcerer's apprentice, has started a process that he cannot stop. Nuclear waste is never got rid of, since reprocessing is incapable of completing the cycle of waste production. Hence the feeling of helplessness suffered by certain technicians at the la Hague plant, who find it very hard, having a job that consists in turning one kind of waste into another kind that, at least for the moment, is equally useless. Exploiting the power of words and the magic of metaphor, those technicians attempt to transmute their work on waste into a useful undertaking for the general good and the plant into a place of sacrifice on a par with the mines of yesteryear. The fact remains that at any moment you may hear this admission that was once made to me: *On laisse de sacrées poubelles pour l'avenir* ('Some fine bloody dustbins we're leaving for the future'). The complaint echoes the nickname of the plant, which no Hagar cares to hear uttered.

A kind of rubbish that can never be got rid of, a poison that will linger for all time, an everlasting blemish, permanent, indomitable pandemonium.

Notes

Introduction: Talking nuclear

1 See P. Ansel, M. H. Barny, J. P. Pages, 'Débat nucléaire et théorie de l'opinion. L'approche de l'opinion publique en France', in *Revue générale nucléaire* 5, 1987, pp. 451–9.

2 On the subject of the euphemisation of risks in an industrial setting, see Christophe Dejours, *Travail: usure mentale*, Paris, Le Centurion, 1980, and Denis Duclos, 'La construction sociale des risques majeurs', in J. L. Fabiani and J. Theys (eds.), *La société vulnérable*, Paris, Presses de l'Ecole normale supérieure, 1988, pp. 37–54.

3 In this branch, the *Confédération française démocratique du travail* (CFDT; a list of the abbreviations used in this book will be found on page xii) has always been the trade union at the forefront of the fight for nuclear safety, and its study of the industry is still authoritative. See Syndicat CFDT de l'Energie atomique, *L'électronucléaire en France*, Paris, Le Seuil, 1975.

4 The liquid effluent from the la Hague nuclear reprocessing plant is discharged into the sea through a five-kilometre pipe. Fishing is prohibited in the vicinity of the outfall. However, the water is warmer at that point and abounds in fish and shellfish, and the word is that a good many fishermen set their lobster pots there!

5 The quotations cited in the text are taken from interviews conducted by myself. I have respected the anonymity of my interviewees, and I have tried so far as possible to preserve their speech patterns.

6 Two people told me they had dreamed of the plant 'blowing up'. One of them was desperately trying to get a job there in order to be able to remain at la Hague. The other, a decontaminator, loathed the work and wanted to quit.

7 I should like to express my gratitude to everyone at la Hague who welcomed me so generously and showed such inexhaustible patience in agreeing to answer the endless questions that I kept firing at them.

8 I should like to thank Mr Delaunay, manager of the COGEMA–la Hague nuclear reprocessing plant, for giving me permission to attend the training course. I should also like to thank the members of the management team who kindly allowed themselves to be interviewed.

1 La Hague or the nuclear zone

1 There is little agreement among archaeologists even today regarding the origins of the Hague-Dicke. Was it a Celtic fortification re-used by the

Vikings, or did the latter build the rampart themselves to shield their war booty? (See M. de Bouard, 'Le Hague-Dicke', in *Cahiers archéologiques*, 1956, VII.)

2 The word *pays* here denotes the territorial units that historically and socially go to make up the Cotentin Peninsula. These are: la Hague, le Val de Saire, le Bauptois, and le Plain. For an account of the recent development of the region, see Colette Muller and Yves Guermond, *Le Cotentin d'aujourd'hui*, Brionne, Gérard Monfort, 1984; J.-J. Berteaux, *Les gens du Cotentin*, Brionne, Gérard Monfort, 1983.

3 The *vent d'amont* blows (often at gale force) from the east and north-east and brings cold, dry weather.

4 A. Dumont, 'Essai sur la natalité dans le canton de Beaumont-Hague', in *Mémoires de la Société d'Anthropologie de Paris*, 1893, third series, Vol. I, Part 1, p. 5.

5 France has three main types of nuclear power station. These are distinguished in terms of their three principal elements:

The fuel, fission of the nuclei of which gives off heat in the reactor core. That fuel may be natural uranium, enriched uranium, or a blend of uranium and plutonium.

The moderator, which is the substance designed to slow the neutrons down in the reactor.

The liquid that carries off the heat required to operate the electricity generators.

The gas-cooled type is the oldest one. Here the moderator is graphite and the coolant carbon dioxide. The fuel is natural uranium. This system has now been abandoned.

The light-water or pressurised-water type of reactor has today taken over from the gas-cooled type. In this, ordinary water serves both as moderator and as coolant. Such stations exist in two types: those that use boiling water (the BWR or boiling-water reactor) and those that use pressurised water (PWR). The fuel used is enriched uranium. Uranium is enriched by increasing its isotope 235 content, the natural composition of the element being approximately 99.3 per cent uranium 238 and 0.7 per cent uranium 235. In France this operation is carried out at Tricastin's Eurodif plant in the Rhône Valley.

The rapid-neutron or fast-breeder reactor represents the most recent technology so far as nuclear power generation is concerned. Water is still the heat-conveying and moderating component. The fuel used is a blend of two fissile materials, plutonium and uranium. The core of the reactor is surrounded by impoverished uranium. This coating captures the neutrons that do not serve to maintain the reaction and turns into plutonium. The fast breeder thus produces more primary nuclear material than it consumes, hence its name.

6 COGEMA, *L'établissement de la Hague aujourd'hui* ('The la Hague plant today'), the brochure handed out to visitors.

7 Given the lifetime of radioactive substances, after 300 years (the time allowed to elapse before storage sites for intermediate-level waste are

returned to civilisation) the radioactivity of these zones will still be one thousandth of a curie per (metric) ton of waste. The report drawn up in 1984 by Professor Castaing, chairman of the Scientific Committee on the Management of Irradiated Fuels, suggested postponing the rehabilitation of these storage sites for several hundred years.

8 For the campaigns fought at Flamanville, the reader is referred to Didier Anger's books, *Chronique d'une lutte*, J.-C. Simoën, 1977, and *Silence, on contamine* (published at the author's expense), 1987.

9 See 'La Hague à l'ère atomique' and 'L'atome au service de la paix', in *La Voix de la Hague*, monthly magazine of the parishes of Beaumont deanery, October, November, December 1960.

10 *Horsain* is a Norman dialect word meaning anyone from outside the municipality.

2 The nuclear setting

1 The plutonium extracted from spent uranium fuel rods cannot be utilised directly in the manufacture of nuclear weapons. It was thought that it could be used as fuel for fast-breeders, but that system has now run into problems. EDF is currently experimenting with a new fuel, MOX, consisting of 4.5 per cent plutonium, at the Saint-Laurent-des-Eaux nuclear power station between Tours and Blois. Its use poses safety and contamination problems that are tricky to resolve. There is consequently little outlet for plutonium. Furthermore, it is difficult and expensive to stockpile. One wonders, in fact, whether it is economically worthwhile to continue reprocessing.

2 For example, a fine study was done by Bernard Paillard (with the collaboration of Claude Fischler) on the Fos-sur-Mer construction site near Marseille, where between 1950 and 1970 an ill-conceived and poorly managed project to build an industrial and dock complex covering twenty-seven square miles had disastrous economic, social, and environmental consequences; see *La damnation de Fos*, Paris, Le Seuil, 1981.

3 *Ouest-France* newspaper, 12 July 1988.

4 The economic, demographic, and social repercussions of the *Grand chantier* are felt throughout the northern part of Manche *département* within a radius of approximately 100 kilometres around Cherbourg.

5 See Françoise Zonabend, 'Une perspective infinie. La terre, le rivage et la mer à la Hague', in *Etudes rurales* 93–4, 1984, pp. 163–78.

6 So far as the management of COGEMA-la Hague is concerned, a candidate is 'local' if at the time of his application he is resident in Manche *département*. For the people of la Hague, 'local' means born in one of the municipalities of the canton.

7 Hélène Puiseux, *L'apocalypse nucléaire et son cinéma*, Paris, Le Cerf, 1987.

8 See M. H. Barny, S. Bonnefous, J. Brenot, 'Huit mois après Tchernobyl. Image du nucléaire', March 1987, Laboratoire de statistiques et d'études économiques et sociales, note 87/05, Commissariat à l'énergie atomique/ Département de Protection sanitaire.

9 'Nucléaire, société et environnement', in *Revue générale du nucléaire* 5, 1987, p. 497.

10 Jean-Jacques Bertaux, *Les gens du Cotentin*, Brionne, Gérard Monfort, 1983, p. 138.
11 From a poem by Cotis Capel, 'La chanson du vent', published in the collection entitled *Les Côtis*, Cherbourg, Edition Isoëte, 1985. The dialect text is:

Caunchoun du vent, ligi, subti,
Et qui sent à-bouon l'avoriblle,
Quaund où R'nouvé verdit l' côtis,
Quaund les flleurs sount enco touot's fîblles.

Caunchoun du vent, caunchoun d'l'hivé,
Du vent qui gent, du vent qui vîpe,
Qu'afoue les houm's, qu'afoue la mé
Dé qui qu' la brôe cache et écllipe.

Caunchoun du vent, caunchoun d' tréjouos,
Qui vyint, qui va, qui crêit, qui moure,
Et qui r'quémench' chaqu' pétié jouo,
J'aim' taount guettyi les nuaes qui couorent.

3 The politics of nuclear power

1 Here I intend to discuss only the civil and political aspects of the nuclear industry's conquest of the region. I shall not (though it is a fascinating subject) be touching on the industrial struggle fought by technicians at the plant both to improve safety standards and to provide better communication at the various levels of the hierarchy. To qualify to tackle these aspects I should have had to spend more time at the plant and been able to attend meetings of the health and safety committees, which was hardly possible.
2 Since the Chernobyl accident and following recommendations from the appropriate body (the Conseil supérieur de la Sûreté et de l'information nucléaire), a scale of values has been drawn up for nuclear events, depending on their relative importance, for the purposes of assessing the severity of the risks involved and keeping the public better informed. The scale is the same as that used to measure the force of earthquakes and is graduated from 1 to 6. The first level of severity covers operating faults with material or human consequences. Levels 2 and 3 include material and human operating incidents, levels 4 and 5 material or human accidents. Level 6 is up in the realm of Chernobyl-type disasters.
   The silo fire of 6 January 1981 measured 4 on the scale and would have justified partial evacuation of la Hague. The fire of 15 April 1980 measured three.
3 *Le Monde*, 8 November 1983 and 2 November 1988.
4 *Condamnés à réussir*, 'a 16 mm colour film about the plant for reprocessing spent nuclear fuel and stockpiling radioactive waste at la Hague (France), produced by the Ciné-Information-Documents collective with the co-operation of the CFDT workers at the plant and the participation of local inhabitants, scientists, and trade-unionists'.

5 A. Collignon, *Le cancer dans le département de la Manche, 1979–1980–1981*, Observatoire régional de la santé de Basse-Normandie et Comité technique régional de cancérologie, Caen, undated.

4 The nuclear site: an inventory of fixtures

1 Société de Travail en Milieu ionisant.

2 The wearing of special clothing is restricted to an hour and a half.

3 'Rem' is another acronym. It stands for 'radium equivalent man' and is a unit of measurement of the radioactive doses received by a person. 1 rem = 1 rad.Q, where Q is a 'quality factor' depending on the organ affected and the different penetrative effects of alpha, beta, and gamma rays, the first being stopped by the skin and the other two passing through the body. In France, maximum permitted annual doses are set at 0.5 rem for the population at large and 5 rems for workers in the nuclear industry.

4 Decret 86–1103 of 2 October 1986 concerning protection of workers against the dangers of ionising radiation.

5 This regulation applies to the COGEMA group. For nuclear power stations and other branches of the nuclear industry it may be different.

5 Learning the nuclear ropes

1 As the fuel is irradiated in a nuclear reactor, *fission products* appear, arising out of the fission of uranium 235 and plutonium 239, as do *transuranic elements*, i.e., elements with an atomic number above 92 (the atomic number of uranium, according to the Mendeleyev table). These elements, for which there is no known industrial use at present, need to be trapped and stockpiled.

2 Half-life: the length of time required for the radioactivity of a substance to be reduced by half.

   Curie (symbol Ci): unit corresponding to the radioactivity of a gram of radium, i.e., 3.7×10^{10} disintegrations per second.

   Becquerel (symbol Bq): unit of radioactivity corresponding to one atomic disintegration per second.

3 Criticity or point of criticity: the point at which a chain reaction is triggered spontaneously. The notion is based on that of *critical mass*. The neutrons generated by the fission of a heavy nucleus may in turn cause further fissions. If only a small amount of fissile material is present, most of the neutrons generated will escape before they can cause fresh fissions. This is what happens in a nuclear reactor. If on the other hand a mass greater than what is called the 'critical mass' is present, the result is a chain reaction that in a very short space of time brings about the fusion of the whole of the fissile mass. This is what happens in a nuclear bomb.

   The critical masses of radioactive substances vary enormously. The plutonium that was formerly used to manufacture nuclear bombs and that was extracted in the early days of the plant had a particularly low critical mass (470 grams is the figure I was given). Hence the need to store and ship plutonium in very special conditions indeed.

The plant is currently geared to producing plutonium for civil use. This is less pure and occurs in the form of plutonium oxide powder, the critical mass of which is around 150 kilograms.

Given that from a metric ton of radioactive waste they extract roughly ten kilograms of this impure plutonium and that certain specific conditions (contact with water, spherical shape, etc.) are required for a chain reaction to be triggered, this event understandably does not head their list of worries at la Hague.

Nevertheless, one wonders why these very simple explanations, which I had to ask for from other technicians, were not provided during the training course.

4 Dose absorbed is the value that represents the energy given up to matter by ionising radiation. Dose equivalent, a value used in radiological protection, takes account of the nature of the ionising radiation and in particular of the way in which the energy is transferred to body tissue, characterised by the quality factor.

For occupational exposure leading to irradiation of the entire organism, the dose equivalent limit has been set at 5 rems for twelve consecutive months, though without exceeding 3 rems per three-month period. Industries may strive (this is what is happening at COGEMA) to get below this threshold.

6   The nuclear everyday

1 The story goes that, before the fast-breeder was started up, certain technicians had expressed doubts about the soundness of certain welds in the tank into which the sodium was to flow. The engineers who had designed the tank simply did not want to know.

2 The (French) Le Robert dictionary defines *fifrelin* as 'small mushroom' or 'trifle, valueless small change'.

3 According to my informant, this expression was imported by workers from the Marcoule reprocessing plant (near Avignon) when they transferred to la Hague.

Among the many meanings of the verb *dauber* are 'to roughcast', 'to insult', 'to strike', and 'to cook meat in a casserole'. Of these the last two may seem apt metaphors for the damage done by radioactivity. I have the impression that, so far as contamination is concerned, the image people have is primarily that of stewed meat. The meaning 'to strike' would fit better with irradiation in the pattern I am describing. However, *daubé* is always used with reference to contamination. In his structural analysis of cooking, Claude Lévi-Strauss of course placed 'boiled' (*le bouilli*) alongside 'rotten' (*le pourri*) (see 'Le triangle culinaire', in *L'Arc* 26, p. 28).

4 'Une émission de rayons lumineux' (*Dictionnaire Le Robert*).

5 'Souillure résultant d'un contact impur' (*Dictionnaire Le Robert*).

6 According to A. Ernout and A. Meillet, *Dictionnaire étymologique de la langue française: Histoire des mots*, Paris, Klincksieck, 1951.

7 Genesis 3:19.

8 See Jean Darriulat, 'La Hague, une usine nucléaire qui vieillit mal' ('a nuclear plant that is ageing badly'), in *Le Matin*, 1979.

9 Emile Benveniste, *Vocabulaire des institutions indo-européennes*, Paris, Minuit, 1969, p. 100.
10 Mary Douglas, *Purity and Disorder*, London, Routledge & Kegan Paul, 1967.
11 The speaker actually used the words *shunter* and *bi-passer*, derived from English (Tr.).
12 This incident gave rise to judicial proceedings in 1978.

Conclusion

1 The reader will find a brief bibliography of these studies in Fabiani and Theys (eds.), *La société vulnérable*, Paris, Presses de l'Ecole normale supérieure, 1988.
2 Mary Douglas and Aaron Wildavsky, *Risk and Culture: An essay on the selection of technological and environmental dangers*, Berkeley, University of California Press, 1983.
3 Denis Duclos, *La peur et le savoir. La société face à la science, la technique et leurs dangers*, Paris, La Découverte, 1989, p. 49.
4 The phrase was coined by Patrick Lagadec as the title of his book: *La civilisation du risque. Catastrophes technologiques et responsabilité sociale*, Paris, Le Seuil, 1981.
5 A statement made to *Le Monde* newspaper on 21 February 1982 by the then manager of the COGEMA-la Hague establishment, Mr Delange.
6 See Gérard Lenclud, 'La tradition n'est plus ce qu'elle était ... Sur les notions de tradition et de société traditionelle en ethnologie', in *Terrain* 9, 1987, pp. 110–23.
7 Eric Stemmelen, 'Le nucléaire dans les structures de l'opinion publique', in *Revue générale du nucléaire* 4, July-August 1983, p. 304.
8 'Les larmes du nucléaire', title of an article in *Le Monde* newspaper, 6 July 1988.
9 'Une ordure éternelle', an expression coined by Professor Pelicier in *Colloque sur les implications psycho-sociologiques du développement de l'industrie nucléaire*, Paris, 13–15 January 1977, published by the Société française de radioprotection, p. 277.
10 See Claude Lévi-Strauss, *Du miel aux cendres*, Paris, Plon, 1966, p. 177.
11 See the article 'Que faire des déchets toxiques?', in *Le Monde diplomatique*, August 1988.
12 Most types of so-called 'high-level' waste have a short half-life. Exceptions are the transuranic elements and plutonium, and the presence of the latter (albeit in tiny quantities) in the end-products of reprocessing cannot be ruled out.

   Indeed, while the quantity of plutonium that should be recovered is fully known when a given quantity of spent fuel is reprocessed, we also know that, at the various stages of reprocessing, losses of plutonium occur. At the la Hague plant, the figures relating to plutonium are kept secret. Which is why, of course, there are always rumours circulating to the effect that 'plutonium pins have gone missing at the plant'.

   This lost plutonium turns up in the 'end-product' waste. It has a half-life of 24,000 years.

Index